Carefree Days

Pran Nevile is a former diplomat and UN adviser. He was born and educated in Lahore. An art historian, he is an acknowledged specialist on the Raj and has also served as a consultant for two BBC films. He is the author of several books. Some of his well-known titles are *Lahore: A Sentimental Journey*, *Nautch Girls of India*, *Beyond the Veil*, *Marvels of Indian Painting* and *K.L. Saigal: The Definitive Biography*. He has compiled and edited *Tribune 125 Years – An Anthology* and *India through American Eyes: 100 Years Ago.*

Also by Pran Nevile

Lahore: A Sentimental Journey

Love Stories from the Raj

Nautch Girls of India

Rare Glimpses of the Raj

Beyond the Veil: Indian Women in the Raj

Stories from the Raj: Sahibs, Memsahibs and Others

K.L. Saigal: Immortal Singer and Superstar

Marvels of Indian Painting

Sahibs' India – Vignettes from the Raj

Raj Revisited

Carefree Days

MANY ROLES, MANY LIVES

Pran Nevile

HarperCollins *Publishers* India

First published in India in 2016 by
HarperCollins *Publishers* India

Building 10, Tower A, 4th Floor, DLF Cyber City, Phase II,
Gurugram Haryana – 122002, India
www.harpercollins.co.in

P-ISBN: 978-93-5177-743-4
E-ISBN: 978-93-5177-744-1

2 4 6 8 10 9 7 5 3 1

Typeset in 12/15 Adobe Garamond Pro
By Saanvi Graphics Noida

Printed and bound at
MicroPrints India, New Delhi

Dedicated with love and respect to
the memory of my parents

Contents

Preface

LAST YEAR, I WAS REPORTED IN print as India's oldest surviving author. This compliment galvanized me to complete my 'memoir' rapidly. I have travelled eighty years into the past to recall the happenings in my long active life. It is a commonplace experience that our remembrance of events that took place fifty to sixty years ago is clearer than recent ones. But this delightful wandering of unfettered thoughts is an enjoyable exercise. Like an old picture, the recollections of early years often become dim and obscure, but some particular events remain so deeply impressed here and there that they defy the effects of time.

As one advances in years, one becomes increasingly detached from the current noise and turmoil, the concerns of the younger generations. I rejoice with the notion that the pleasant days of my long life are not over yet, and look forward to every dawn with delight and hope for some new thrill and joy.

Practically all my contemporaries, comrades and colleagues have already departed for the popularly termed heavenly abode. Those close to my fading age group often wish for dying in sleep, not realizing that death itself is a sleep in which there are no dreams.

The foregoing is not a relevant preface but then it is the last part of a book to be written, and is seldom read. All the same, the gentle reader should know something about this memoir. During more than seventy years of my multi-professional working life, I have been a journalist, research official, public sector manager, bureaucrat, economic diplomat, Soviet bloc expert, UNCTAD (United Nations Conference on Trade and Development) adviser, freelance writer and author, art historian, chronicler of the Raj era, and protagonist of people's music, which is my chief occupation at present. In this memoir, an effort has been made to narrate the story of my multi-professional, eventful as well as colourful life, which has been acclaimed as unusual and extraordinary.

I have done most of my writings in the congenial atmosphere of the India International Centre (IIC) library. I would like to express sincere appreciation for all the courtesies and assistance extended to me in my work by Dr S. Majumdar, chief librarian, and his team, especially Shefali Bhatt and Rajeev Mishra.

For the musical functions organized by me over the years I am deeply grateful to Premola Ghose, chief of Programme Division, IIC, and her colleague L.S. Tochhawng. Also, I would like to thank Shadab Hussain, Dr Chandrima Majumdar and Aditi Chauhan of India Habitat Centre (IHC) and Epicentre for their help in holding these functions. Sincere thanks are offered to Shalini Bhargava for critical appraisal of the functions and valuable suggestions.

I would like to mention that the idea of writing a memoir was initially planted in my mind by my eldest grandson Ravi and enthusiastically supported by other grandchildren Gaurika, Aditya and Anshuman. I am grateful to Madeeha Gauhar for her valuable suggestion to include a chapter on the Partition. Thanks should also go to Humra Quraishi for prodding me to complete this book as soon as possible. Further, I owe the greatest debt to my wife Savitri for her unflagging support throughout, until her passing away in 2013. I am also indebted to my daughters-in-law Madhulika and Megha for going through the manuscript and their overall assistance.

Finally, my grateful thanks go to HarperCollins Publishers and their former CEO, P.M. Sukumar, for evincing interest in my work. Special thanks are also due to Krishan Chopra and his team for their abiding interest in monitoring the progress of the book as well as his help and guidance in organizing its timely publication.

Gurgaon
February 2016

Pran Nevile

1

Early Years

I HAIL FROM A SMALL LANDOWNING family, and my grandfather, a Sanskrit scholar and astrologer, supplemented his income by teaching and training boys in the conduct of religious rituals and ceremonies, and preparing them for the priestly profession. My father, the eldest son, was one of the early boys to move to a town for high school education. Fortunately, he had an aunt living in Jalandhar, where he went after his middle school and passed the entrance (matriculation) examination. He was keen to study further but was unable to do so due to lack of resources and took employment in the postal department at Lahore. He was the first member of the family to turn a city dweller. I was born in 1922, nearly a decade after his moving to Lahore.

My earliest memory takes me back to my ancestral village Vairowal in Amritsar district. It was a unique village with several pucca houses and even brick-paved streets. It had a dharmashala with its own well that supplied drinkable water. This unusual environment of the village was attributed to the fact that Maharaja Ranjit Singh used to camp here during his hunting excursions.

Vairowal boasted of a post office and middle school. It was dominated by the Sikh community of Bawa clan, who claimed their descent from Guru Angad Dev. Then there were some Hindu families and also Muslims who asserted their Rajput origin. The village residents were mostly landowners, big and small, who had leased out their lands to cultivators under the batai (crop sharing) system, which ensured a sizeable share for the landowners. The village was reasonably prosperous until the last decade of the nineteenth century, when the new generation started moving out to urban centres of Punjab in search of employment. The successive fragmentation of landholdings through inheritance made it difficult for families to survive with shrinking land income. Located in the heart of 'Maja' segment of Punjab, the people of Vairowal had an inborn trait of enterprise and adventure. No wonder some of them settled in distant lands across the seas, thanks to the British colonial masters.

I vaguely remember my early childhood days when we lived in a rented house in Mohalla Mohlian inside Lahori Gate of the walled city. A four-storeyed structure, it was the tallest in the neighbourhood. There was then neither electricity nor house taps. Misars (professional water carriers) delivered water in large vessels from nearby wells, charging six annas (37 paise of today) per vessel on a monthly basis. For light, we managed with kerosene lamps of different shapes and sizes, the most common being the portable hurricane lamp of English make. The streets were also lighted with kerosene lamps, installed by the municipal committee, whose workers used to light them every evening and turn them off in the morning. By the 1930s we had electricity in the house. I vividly remember the landmarks of the neighbourhood. There was a popular akhara (wrestlers' arena) run by one Gokal Pandit, who trained young wrestlers but was more known in the city for running a clinic for birds, treating those injured by the sharp twine of flying kites. Nearby was a cluster of Muslim professional printers of textile materials with their wooden blocks. Lahore boasted of a friendly division of occupations. The entire vegetable and fruit trade, and the bulk supply of milk to the city's halwais (milk and sweets vendors), mostly Hindus, were handled by Muslims who were also skilled craftsmen. An enterprising Muslim lady in our mohalla ran a tailoring shop at her house and womenfolk of all communities, wanting to avoid male tailors, flocked to her. Kite making, a big business in Lahore, was dominated by Muslims who were experts in the art.

Another thing vivid in my memory is the horde of street vendors adding gaiety to day-to-day life. They offered a wide range of wares from fruits, vegetables, eatables, textile materials, knives and scissors, to cosmetics. An interesting practice was the bartering of old garments and shoes for metal utensils. Then there was the workman, the kalayiwala (tin plater) who would set up his mini workshop with fire and a collapsible blower and loudly announce his presence. It was customary to have brass utensils tinned time to time when the plating had worn off. Perched near the windows above, womenfolk enjoyed bargaining with vendors and took delivery of things with their chhikas (baskets with strings) lowered down to reach the vendor.

Returning to my story: a child's admission to school in those days was an occasion for celebration and sweets were distributed among friends and relations. This was done in my case too when I joined Sanatan Dharm Middle School, housed in a large haveli in Wachhowali Bazar. Within the school premises stood a temple in the vast courtyard where worshippers would assemble for evening prayers. A section of the building was set apart for a Sanskrit Pathshala (teaching house), where the vidyarthis (students) undertook the study of Sanskrit and prepared for the Prajna, Visharad and Shastri examinations. The morning prayer, led by one of the teachers and some senior schoolboys, was the first activity of the day. Boys stood in rows and repeated 'Jai Jagadish Hare' after the teacher. We greeted the teachers with 'Jai Sita Ram' and repeated it at the time of roll-call. First-grade class was held in the open courtyard and children sat on reed mats spread on the floor. During winter, the class was shifted to the terrace on the third floor in warm sunshine. In the event of occasional rain, the class was dismissed and children were happy to go home. It normally took two years to pass the first grade, which was divided into two parts called kachchi (preliminary) and pukki (secondary). The children of primary classes carried to school a takhti or patti, a rectangular wooden board with a small triangular handle, a reed pen and an earthen inkpot containing a rag piece soaked in black ink. The takhti, which served as a writing board, had to be washed daily and coated with gachi (earthen paste). It was an amusing sight to watch children drying takhtis at the furnaces of halwais. After the fourth grade, takhtis were replaced with slates and exercise books. We recited multiplication tables in a sing-song manner to memorize them.

The headmaster of the school, Lala Panju Mal, and his team of teachers were a devoted lot who not only imparted knowledge to their pupils but also taught them moral values. Lapses in studies and behaviour were punished. 'Spare the rod and spoil the child' was the accepted dictum. Children were taught to respect their teachers and parents, and even when spared for any lapses at home, they were bound to be punished at school.

After passing out from middle school I joined the Dayanand Anglo-Vedic (DAV) High School founded in memory of Swami Dayanand Saraswati, the founder of Arya Samaj. In those days seeking admission to any school of one's own choice was no problem. DAV School was famous all over Punjab, with its students winning top positions year after year in the matriculation examination. The school covered a vast expanse of land and boasted of having a gymnasium, a swimming pool and up-to-date laboratories equipped with burners fed through piped gas. Headed by Lala Suraj Bhan, the school had a team of distinguished teachers, some of whom were authors of textbooks. Special classes were conducted for a select group of brilliant students appearing for the matriculation examination, and they were even served milk and eatables at the school's expense.

An interesting feature of Arya Samaj teaching was the stress it laid on brahmacharya (celibacy) and moral character. Prominently displayed on billboards hung on the walls of the school hall were such dictums:

> When wealth is lost, nothing is lost.
> When health is lost, something is lost.
> When character is lost, everything is lost.

The education system, designed to make us good citizens of the British Empire, laid stress on the study of English life and letters. It was imperative to study the 'Blessings of British Rule' as this question was a must in examinations. I recall how we had mugged up an ideal answer. It began like this: 'What a marvellous change has the comparatively short period of British Rule brought about! An age of violence and rapine has given place to one of peace and harmony, an age of ignorance has been followed by one of enlightenment.'

The medium of instruction in schools was chiefly Urdu; English being compulsory from fourth grade onwards. It is interesting to note that the Punjabi language did not figure at all in the school curriculum. For us it was only a spoken language. Unlike other Indian provinces, where the medium of instruction was the mother tongue, Urdu was imposed in Punjab – both as an official language up to the district level and the medium of instruction in schools. The reason for this was that after annexing Punjab, British rulers found that educated and literate Punjabis were familiar with Urdu script since the entire Punjabi literature was in this script. Besides, the John Company officials who came to administer Punjab had working knowledge of Urdu, having served in the region of present-day Uttar Pradesh and Bihar.

The announcement of matriculation results in the first week of May was a notable event in the city. The results were published in the *Tribune*, an English daily. Friends and relations would gather to congratulate the successful candidates who would distribute sweets to celebrate the occasion. When my matriculation results came out, I was thrilled to find that not only had I won a scholarship but had also, scoring 703 marks out of 850, secured the third rank out of the 26,000 students who had appeared in the University of Punjab. Incidentally, in those days the university offered forty scholarships strictly on the basis of marks and these carried a monthly stipend of Rs 18 – a big sum in those days. Lahore, being the leading centre of education in north India, attracted students from all over Punjab, NWFP (North-West Frontier Province), Jammu and Kashmir (J&K), and even Delhi. The city had many colleges, the most prestigious being the Government College. Only highly meritorious students could hope to join it, though scions of landlords, title-holders and high government officials were given preference.

My admission to the college was purely on merit. The magnificent Gothic edifice of the college, occupying a commanding site, was a landmark of Lahore. It was designed by W. Purdon CE, and constructed by Rai Kanhya Lal, CE, at a cost of Rs 3,20,000 in 1877. One of the first things that struck me was the cosmopolitan atmosphere of the college, there being no communal divide amongst students. Hindu and Muslim boys mixed freely in a friendly atmosphere. They lived together in two college hostels: the 'Quadrangle' and 'New Hostel'. There were, however, separate kitchens for the Hindu and Muslim boarders, though they freely exchanged dishes with one another. With G.D. Sondhi as principal, the faculty boasted of professors and lecturers with an Oxford or Cambridge background. They were all elegantly dressed, donned black gowns and would majestically enter classrooms to deliver lectures. A few of them, instead of lecturing, dictated notes from old, worn-out notebooks while others would encourage a dialogue with students and enliven their lectures with spicy anecdotes.

There was practically no social interaction with the opposite sex. It was always a delightful experience to see a few well-groomed Punjabi girls walking in the campus. Some students used to loiter outside girls' colleges trying to attract the attention of pretty faces. It was a simple, innocent pleasure, unspoilt by eve-teasing. There were a few who would pen Urdu verses in praise of girls they silently admired without ever exchanging a word with them. Some others would pen down love letters to their imaginary girlfriends, the popular opening sentence being: 'Sorry to upset your mind, which is bound to be perplexed at the sight of this letter which bears a hand quite foreign to your eyes.'

Going to the hills during summer vacations was a status symbol. The popular resorts were Simla and Mussoorie. I have fond memories of my two-month sojourn at Mussoorie in 1938 with my classmate and friend Balkrishan Joshi. We persuaded our parents to send us there for pursuing our studies for the final intermediate examination in the cool hills. The most enjoyable diversion in Mussoorie was horse riding. It cost only eight annas (half a rupee) per hour. The next was a holiday trip to Kashmir in 1939 with two friends, Narottam Berry and Inder Jolly. It was our maiden visit to the picturesque paradise we had heard so much about. We made it all the more memorable by doing a pilgrimage to the sacred Amarnath cave, considered to be the most arduous among Hindu pilgrimage centres. We covered the entire journey on foot from Pahalgam up to Amarnath, crossing snow bridges and hilltops rising over 15,000 ft. It took us three days with night stopovers at Chandanwari, Sheshnag and Panchtarni. All the same, we felt a sense of achievement and took pride in narrating the adventurous travel to our friends. Another joyful travel of student days was in December 1941 – a university-sponsored trip for MA (economics) students to Bombay for attending the 'All India Economic Conference'. The North Western Railways provided us, a group of twenty students, one full bogie which served as our lodging as well. It was detached and kept on the railways sidings at different stations en route. After leaving Lahore we visited Delhi, Jaipur, Mount Abu, Ahmedabad and Baroda, spending a couple of days at each place before reaching our destination. There the owner of Ram Lal Silk Mills, an industrialist from Punjab, played host and put us up in his comfortable guest house with all facilities, including a lavish breakfast. This trip was indeed the most educative, exciting and unforgettable experience of my student days.

My last jaunt as a student was in Simla – the imperial summer capital. Indian hill stations are among the notable relics of the Raj, with Simla occupying pride of place. I was there during my summer vacation in 1942, when everybody was talking about World War II, which the Japanese had brought to India's doorstep. This was the last summer when the viceroy and the government staff were lending importance to the city since thereafter the annual summer move to Simla was discontinued as a measure of economy. I had a two-month escape from the searing heat of Lahore and saw Simla in its full imperial glory.

Finally, the day arrived to bid farewell to my enjoyable student life. It was in 1943 when, having graduated, I paid my last visit to the college to collect an important document – the character certificate – signed by Principal G.D. Sondhi. It was a standard form listing a student's academic performance and his participation in sports and other extramural activities, followed by general remarks. These were considered to be of great relevance, especially for government service, which was in those days the ultimate goal for many of us from middle-class families.

I merited the following remarks:

'Mr Pran Nath has had a brilliant academic career and is an all-round first class man. He has a pleasing personality and is thoroughly suitable for any government service for which his academic qualifications fit him.'

2

Carefree Days in Lahore

IN THE LAHORE OF MY DAYS, there were plenty of games and pastimes, fairs and festivals, recreations and diversions to keep us amused all year round. We had to just walk into the street to be entertained by madaris (magicians), bazigars (acrobats), bhands (jesters), animal and bird tamers, snake charmers, folk singers, not to forget Chinese gymnasts who would be out on their daily rounds. The monotony of life was relieved by these joyful amusements and people had enough time to stand and stare. Lahore, like a magnet, had drawn them to its environs and kept them happy by its generous patronage.

As children we, both boys and girls, played together with earthenware toys and wooden gaind-balla (ball and bat), shared the peeng or jhula jhulna (swing) and competed in kirhi-kahra, a game in which the participants jump on one leg, pushing a piece of stone through a rectangular area divided into eight sections drawn on the floor with charcoal or chalk. Another favourite game was lukamchai or hide-and-seek, in which children would hide and one of them pursued while singing, '*Luk chhip jana, makai da dana, raje di beti aai ai*'. Up to the age of eight or nine, boys were allowed to play with girls. Thereafter they played different games. The boys moved on to gulli-danda and kanchas (marbles) while the girls took to playing with dolls, gitas or tiny stone pieces, and skipping. The boys' gulli-danda is a sport that demands a quick reflex, exceptional hand-eye coordination, strong wrists and a powerful grasp.

Similarly, playing with kanchas or shooting small marbles involves placing a marble ball against the tip of the left forefinger, which is drawn back and quickly released so as to hit the ball against which the blow is intended. The game demands the ability to judge distances and strike the target with precision.

Kite flying was then an extremely popular sport and Lahore was hailed as the kite flying capital of the world. I cannot recall anything more thrilling than kite flying in my boyhood. Whenever I observed my kite soaring towards the clouds, I experienced a sense of power and mastery over the elements. Perhaps, in a way, I identified myself with the kite flying so free and so high above me, far from the madding crowd, enveloping me in a spirit of freedom and adventure. I felt that kites signified hope, a desire for escape, fancy dreams entrusted to a breath of wind, connected to a string and the hand that clasped it. Those were the days when kite fighting instead of kite flying was in vogue. Paicha larhana or to entrap another kite by pouncing upon it from above or below or sideways, depending on its position, was the most exciting part of the sport. The skill lay in crossing the dore (twine) with an opponent's until the vanquished kite, cut loose, floated helplessly over the rooftops. The victor and his teammates would announce the defeat of the rival with loud cries of Bo-kata and throw a challenge for a return paicha. The defeated rival would accept the challenge and stir up a fresh kite into the sky. The rules of the game did not permit entrapping a kite till it was high above in the sky. It required great manoeuvring to entangle or disentangle one's kite from the clutches of the opponent. Sometimes, we heard a shrill commotion on the rooftops and saw boys running with bamboo poles to catch a drifting kite. The falling kite in a street or bazaar created a stir and passersby of all ages would run to catch the booty. Some boys, who could not afford to buy kites, often amused themselves by watching kite fights and catching the fallen kites. We always looked forward to Basant, the kite-flying festival during January–February, when thousands of kites of different shapes and sizes would sail in the sky and rooftops crowded with fliers and spectators.

Festivals and fairs, which provided a delightful diversion for people, were also events of social significance. Celebrated with pomp and show – Lorhi, Basant, Holi, Baisakhi, Dussehra, Diwali, Id, Moharram and Gurpurav – were symbols of a composite culture, and all communities participated in them. Religious processions attracted large crowds of people who would line up in bazaars and stand on balconies of houses to be able to witness them. The great attraction was the procession of jhankis or floats elaborately set up on bullock carts with a miniature stage where amateur artists would enact incidents from the Ramayana. Some of the jhankis depicted colourful scenes from the epic. Seated on them were singers who entertained the surging crowds. The onlookers used to occupy vantage points in bazaars, hours before the arrival of the processions, and kept a night vigil to witness the full show, which usually concluded at dawn. People spent lavishly during the festivals which promoted communal harmony.

The festivals were also occasions for holding dangals (wrestling matches), which carried attractive prizes. Kushti (wrestling) was a popular sport and a number of akharas (wrestling grounds) were run by renowned pehalwans (wrestlers) in different parts of the city. It required several years of hard training to become a pehalwan and also a special diet of energy-yielding almonds and milk products. The pehalwans of Lahore were famous all over the country for their physical strength and ingenious daos (holds) to defeat the adversary. Wrestling matches were held in the open air before a large assembly of people. The moment one of the wrestlers succeeded in knocking his adversary flat on his back, he was declared the victor and loud cries of 'wah, wah' (bravo) from the enthusiastic and admiring multitude would fill the air. The victor was lifted and, riding on the shoulders of one of his supporters, was carried triumphantly, followed by a band of musicians. The spectators on their part would crown him with wreaths of flowers. The city was proud of Rustam-e-Zaman (the world champion) Gama Pehalwan, who defeated Zbysko at Patiala in 1928.

Another kind of entertainment was provided by travelling circuses and carnival companies when they visited Lahore. Circus shows were a novelty and attracted people of all ages. Carnivals offered a veritable feast for gamblers until these were banned by the government in the mid-1930s. Carnival companies had the added attraction of amusement parks with giant wheels, swings, merry-go-rounds, etc. These amusement parks were later merged with the periodic exhibitions held at Lahore. A wonder that appeared on the scene in 1935 was the dodgem car and I still remember how impatiently I had stood in the queue to take my turn. Consisting of small electrically powered cars, riders would drive and try to bump other cars while avoiding being bumped by others. It was a thrilling experience, which in those days cost four annas (one-fourth of a rupee) for a ten-minute ride. Many a daring feat was shown on these occasions. I recall a couple of them that created a sensation in the city. One was the driving of a motorcycle on the walls of a specially constructed wooden well, called the well of death, and the other was a daring jump into a water tank from a height of 65 feet by a stuntman after setting himself aflame.

I vividly remember my maiden visit to a cinema house to watch a silent film, *Chandramukhi*, starring Miss Gohar. This was in 1930, when as a child I wondered what exciting things would appear on the screen. My uncle, who had secured some complimentary passes, took me inside the long hall of Paris Cinema, which had a roof of corrugated steel sheets. There was much hustle-bustle with vendors moving about all over the hall selling cigarettes and eatables: boiled eggs, peanuts, chilgozas, sugar candy, etc. The management rang the bell three times before starting the show. With the final call, vendors quit the hall and viewers occupied their seats. Instead of dialogues, written titles flashed on the screen which many in the audience read aloud. A few musicians sat near the screen and played their instruments whenever there was a hilarious, sad or romantic scene, or a sword fight.

The advent of talkies in 1931 brought about a revolution in the entertainment scene of Lahore. The novelty of sound began attracting larger crowds to cinema houses. I fondly remember watching the first talkie *Radha Rani* in 1932. Produced by Ranjit Film Co., Bombay, and starring singer-actors Miss Gohar and Master Bhagwandas, it was a big hit. Then I remember seeing some other films like *Laila Majnu*, *Shirin Farhad*, *Shakuntala* and *Nal Damayanti*, all starring the then famous duo – Master Nissar and Miss Kajjan. As a young boy I enjoyed watching stunt films like *Hunterwali* and *Toofan Mail* starring the famous Miss Nadia. But as I grew older, I was drawn to movies with popular music and romantic themes. The leading producers in this field were New Theatres, Calcutta; Bombay Talkies; Prabhat Film Co.,Pune; and Minerva Studios, Bombay. I remember the box office hits of those days: *Devdas*, *Vidyapati*, *Achhut Kanya*, *Amar Jyoti*, *Pukar* and *Sikandar*. The leading stars then were K.L. Saigal, Ashok Kumar, Prithviraj, Chandarmohan and Sohrab Modi. The heroines were Kananbala, Devika Rani, Shanta Apte, Durga Khote and Naseem

Bano. It was around 1940 that Lahore studios came to life and ventured into the production of Punjabi and Hindi films. The first great Hindi hit was *Khazanchi* in 1941, which created a sensation with its haunting music loaded with Punjabi folklore.

As college students, we got interested in English movies as well. While some of us wanted to learn more about spoken English, others were keen on watching provocative love scenes not available in Hindi movies. The outstanding English movies of those days still etched in my memory are *The Adventures of Robin Hood, How Green Was My Valley, Lady of the Tropics, Gone with the Wind, Rebecca, Lady Hamilton, All This and Heaven Too* and *Gaslight*. It was then fashionable to talk about English movies and famous Hollywood stars like Errol Flynn, Gary Cooper, Robert Taylor, Ronald Coleman, Charles Boyer, Clark Gable, Gregory Peck and Laurence Olivier. The leading actresses included Hedy Lamarr, Greta Garbo, Olivia de Havilland, Maureen O'Hara, Marlene Dietrich, Rita Hayworth and Ginger Rogers.

The novel idea of combining a film show with '*zinda nach te gana*', (live dance and song performance) came up in late 1930s. Film production could not provide new releases for the increasing number of cinema houses and some of them had to depend on second-run films. This impelled them to provide an added attraction in the form of live dance-and-song performances in order to pull the crowds, where they offered '*ek ticket mein do maze*'(two enjoyments for the price of one).

I recall watching a live dance-and-song performance by Miss Sarla and her troupe along with the Ranjit Movietone film *Bhola Shikar* starring Mehtab and E. Billimoria. It was announced that Miss Sarla and her troupe had come from the Bombay film world but the fact was that she hailed from Hira Mandi, the red-light district of Lahore. Having seen the film already, I was keen to see the live performance. The screening of the film was interrupted only after the audience became restive, whistling and shouting for Sarla's appearance. The stage was then lit and musicians seated themselves in a corner and began playing the harmonium, tabla, and sarangi. Then followed the deafening beat of a drum behind the stage, announcing the appearance of Miss Sarla, the dancing star. Her veiled arm could now be seen from the right end of the stage. In an instant she leapt out with a burst of song, like a flash of lightning from behind a darkening cloud. Such was the dramatic effect created by her appearance and the melodious sound of ghungroos and strains aired by the musicians that the hall resounded with applause. She had uttered the opening lines of a song which was on the lips of every Punjabi in those days, '*Palla mar ke bujha gayi diwa – ke akh nal gal kar gayi chhayi*' (she put out the lamp with a jerk of her veil and conveyed a message through her eyes). Whirling and swaying, Sarla wove her spell with tinkling feet and the rhythmic movement of her arms and hands, emphasizing the meaning of the song. Beginning with the fingertips, her whole hand took up the rhythm. She danced with elegance and ease, her movements expressing love, joy, hope, despair or jealousy in tune with the lyrics of the song.

Responding to the loud applause of 'mukarar' (say it again) from the audience, Sarla advanced gracefully towards the front of the stage. With the burst of a song she turned around with such vigour that the loose folds of her gown expanded and the heavily embroidered border, with which it was trimmed, fanned out from her waist, showing for an instant the alluring outline of her lower form. She displayed remarkable muscle control and coordination as she worked herself up to reach the climax of her dance. The audience burst out in applause, which manifested itself not only in loud clapping but also in showering of coins on to the stage. The tinkling sound of the coins drove the musicians to a new pitch of enthusiasm just as Miss Sarla made her exit. The repeated requests of 'once more' and another shower of coins from the audience persuaded her to make another appearance to salaam and acknowledge the applause.

As students, after crossing eighteen, we considered ourselves adults ready to get acquainted with the sex trade and its practitioners. Some of our seniors often boasted about enjoying with young beauties not from Hira Mandi, but from other lesser-frequented quarters of Lahore. There the sex trade operated privately for the gentry, which shunned going to the well-known Hira Mandi. They also informed us about the famous pimp 'Fazal', who carried on his business, walking up and down on McLeod Road opposite Palace Cinema. One evening, my friend Saeed and I went there to gather experience. I would like to narrate a graphic account of our encounter with Fazal and the subsequent adventure.

'Fazal...Fazal...Fazal.'

We heard this name being called but could see no one around except a man wrapped in a shawl walking in the opposite direction.

Soon he turned around, approached us and enquired,'Bauji, did you call me?' We were quite surprised; the cry of Fazal had come from his direction. Apparently, he was shouting his own name.

When we said that we hadn't called anybody, he at once changed the subject, and said, 'Forget about it. By the way, what are you up to at this time of the evening? Bauji, I can make your evening unforgettable if you come with me.'

'Where to?'

'Not far off.'

'What for?'

'You appear to be quite innocent. I know a number of your college mates. Have you not heard my name from them? I know you are all afraid of going to Hira Mandi. I can assure you there is nothing to fear. I will show you sparkling beauties who have just arrived from Sargodha. If you like, you can spend time with any of them, otherwise you come back. No hard feelings. In fact, my patrons include the rich and famous of Lahore. I provide my services to the gentry and enjoy meeting young pleasure seekers like you.'

'Where is this place?'

'About 200 yards from Prabhat Cinema. You can deposit your cycles at the Palace cycle stand and come with me in a tonga.'

'How much will it cost to have one go?'

'Bauji, it all depends on the grace and charm of the maal (girl).'

'Suppose we don't like any of the girls?'

'Then just pay me one rupee, inclusive of tonga hire. This you have to pay in advance.'

'Is this place quite safe? I mean there is no risk of a police raid?'

'Bauji, have a look at my grey hair. Don't imagine they have taken this hue through exposure to the sun.'

'Anyway, it is better to be cautious. By the way, we hope you will show us only young things. We are not game for middle-aged stuff.'

'Bauji, all of them are like toys of sugar, with pink cheeks, silken hair and pear-shaped breasts. They are new to the profession but well trained in manners and the art of making love. You will have a taste of paradise when they cling to you like lizards.'

As soon as we sat on the rear seat of the tonga, we felt nervous. Turning our faces away from the gaze of the passersby, we tried to put on a bold face, but could not hide the state of our mind from Fazal, who was quietly watching us from the front seat where he sat with the tonga driver. We continued to feel uneasy as the journey seemed to be never-ending. Soon, we saw the tonga turning into a dark by-lane. Our heartbeats quickened. After a few more turns, we stopped in front of a dilapidated house. Fazal asked us to get down from the tonga and wait on the roadside. We saw him going up a dark, unlit staircase. We were now getting more frightened and regretted our decision to come there. Soon we heard the sound of someone coming down the steps. Fazal was there, all smiles and ready to guide us upstairs. We followed him nervously and soon found ourselves in a dark room with a table lamp placed in a corner, emitting a glimmer of light through its 5-candlepower bulb. There were no tables or chairs, only a webbing cot covered with a black-and-white khes (thick sheet). Fazal asked us to sit down on the cot and feel at home. We were told to sit in the right and left corners of the cot leaving its middle vacant. We were getting tense and jittery. Then we heard the sound of clinking glass bangles and female voices in the adjoining room. In a moment, Fazal shouted, '*Chheti karo, kudiyo*,' (hurry up, girls) and then appeared the first of the beauties walking slowly towards us. She sat between us on the cot. She wore a green satin long shirt and salwar with a red chunni, half covering her black greasy hair. She wore an over-sized nose ring, which instead of enhancing her charm diminished it. In that dim light, her wheatish complexion and unremarkable looks failed to enthuse us.

Fazal had already made it clear that we were not to touch any part of her body. He asked Mahtab to talk to us. Whereupon, she smiled and as she leaned back, her chunni slipped down from her bosom. This provided us with a good view of her breasts but their very sight disappointed us. It was a far cry from the pear-shaped bosom described to us by Fazal. We signalled to Fazal that we would like to go, indicating our disapproval. Fazal asked Mahtab to retire and send in Shanti. In a few moments Shanti descended in our midst. We began our physical survey of Shanti while Fazal started narrating, obviously with the aim of influencing our selection, her background and how she had landed in this pleasure nest. Shanti hailed from Pangi Valley in Chamba, famous for its bevy of beauties all over the country. Her sister Phoolan had been picked up by men of the Maharaja of Patiala and placed in his 'harem'. But Shanti was enamoured by Lahore.

Fair and voluptuous, Shanti wore tight white pyjamas and an orange long shirt. She was quite fleshy, though not at the right places. My friend whispered in my ear that she was too plump. But her bold eyes were highly seductive and it seemed she could talk through them. She had green dots tattooed on her chin; her fingertips, the palms of her hands, toes and the soles of her feet were tinted with henna; her lips were stained brownish red with dentifrice, and in the centre of her forehead she bore a little mark in red which served as a beauty spot.

Without waiting for any signal from us, Fazal called out for Gulshan to appear. Shanti retired but not without giving us wanton smiles and languishing glances. Her place was now taken by Gulshan. Fazal suddenly switched over to speaking in Urdu from Punjabi, describing her as a unique 'piece' from Meerut having a Mughal lineage. She wore a pink garrara (wide-bottomed pyjamas), a white silk shirt and a red dupatta. Richly oiled, her hair was neatly parted in the middle and a long, thick plait dangled over her breasts, showing the enormous length of her jet-black locks. Her eyelids and brows were darkened, which accentuated the size of her eyes and gave them a lustrous appearance. Though somewhat dark in complexion, Gulshan created a favourable impression on us. We now started comparing the merits of the three beauties displayed before us. Fazal signalled Gulshan to depart and enquired about our choice.

'Bauji, I know it is extremely difficult to make a choice because all three are equally worth enjoying.'

'How much for one go?'

'Bauji, a very special concession for students like you, just make your choice quickly. One of you can make your love nest in this room and the other in the adjoining one while I wait for you downstairs.'

'But still, how much do we have to pay?'

'Bauji, five rupees each, and if fully satisfied, you may give some reward to your humble servant, Fazal. I have not the least doubt you will be more than happy and always remember Fazal thereafter.' The price quoted was within our means, and while we were gathering enough courage to make our selection known, we were startled by the sound of someone's steps on the staircase. We panicked, ran out of the room, and rushed down to the street. Fazal followed us and soon caught up with us at the street corner.

'Bauji, what is wrong? You appear to be frightened. Why did you leave all of a sudden?'

'That stranger unnerved us.'

'Oh Bauji, you both are too simple. You only know how to talk and not how to act.'

'But who is that stranger?'

'He is Mahtab's cousin and stays in the house. He is a family member and runs the establishment. He has his separate room on the terrace and doesn't disturb anybody. Bauji, have faith in me. There is nothing to worry about. Let us return. You should amuse yourself after all this trouble.'

I realized that we were being timid and lacked the courage to proceed with this sexual adventure. My thumping heart told me to run away from the place.

Somehow I composed myself and said, 'Fazal Mian, *aj rain de, kuch* mood *nahin banya*' (Let it be today, we are not in a proper mood). We felt guilty that we had wasted so much of Fazal's time. In order to avoid Fazal carrying a poor impression of us and to cover up our timidity, I gave two one-rupee coins to him, telling him we were really delighted and would surely use his services next time.

Fazal accepted the money, repeated his suggestion to return but noting our reluctance bade us goodbye and said, '*Bauji, kuch swad nahin aaya, achchha koi gal nahin, agli wari raunak lawange*' (It has been rather disappointing but doesn't matter, next time there will be a lively celebration).

As we were returning, I was reminded of a popular couplet, '*Baha ke yaar ko pehlu mein raat bhar sahir, jo kuch nahin karte wo kamal karte hai*' (With one's beloved in the lap for the whole night, those who do nothing are lauded for their marvellous achievement).

3

Press Information Bureau

HAILING FROM AN EDUCATED MIDDLE-CLASS FAMILY, government service was then the principal goal in life. There was limited scope in the private sector and without suitable recommendation one could not hope to get in there. After obtaining an MA degree in economics, I had dreamt of doing my PhD from the London School of Economics but it was not possible to go there during the war. With my commendable academic record, I got the post of a lecturer in DAV College, Hoshiarpur. When I visited the town I found it to be rather dull and dreary. It lacked the metropolitan ambience of Lahore which I was used to. So I politely declined the offer. There were ample opportunities during the war to join the armed forces and a number of my classmates had got emergency commissions in the army, air force and navy. But temperamentally I was not cut out for a military career. There was keen competition for technical posts in the Department of Information and Broadcasting (I&B). Responding to an advertisement in newspapers, I applied for the post of an assistant journalist in the Bureau of Public Information, later designated as Press Information Bureau (PIB). After a competitive test and interview I was selected and joined the PIB on 22 July 1944. It was an attached office to the I&B department, then headed by the secretary, G.S. Bozman, ICS.

I have vivid memories of my first day in office, located on the second floor of the North Block. Its entry was from the famous Jalebi Chowk with its large cycle stand and a small hutment housing the photo section of the PIB. I was assigned to the 'newspaper section' under the charge of R.K. Chatterjee and entrusted with the task of preparing daily 'round-ups of press comments' carried by leading English newspapers as well as weekly and monthly journals. I enjoyed doing this work as it enriched my knowledge of day-to-day political and economic developments in the country. These 'round-ups' were duly classified and sent to the PIB's information officers who forwarded them with their remarks to the departments concerned. All government news was transmitted to the print media through press notes issued by the PIB. Taking note of my economics qualification, I was later assigned the task of collecting economic and commercial information and preparing background notes for press releases. I recall how I went through each and every page of journals like *Commerce*, *Indian Finance*, *Eastern Economist* and the *Capital*. This kept me abreast of the developments in the field of Indian trade and industry, and helped me in my later years in the commerce ministry.

The PIB was headed by the principal information officer (PIO), J. Natarajan, the first Indian to occupy this post. A gentleman to the core, he had no airs and was kind and generous in his behaviour towards everyone irrespective of his rank and position. I vividly remember his farewell party and the group photograph with the entire PIB staff in 1945. He was succeeded by A.S. Iyengar. Next in hierarchy were the deputy principal information officers followed by information officers, assistant information officers, journalists and assistant journalists. These were all technical posts. The supporting staff of clerks, assistants and superintendents belonged to the ministerial service of the Government of India, later christened as the Central Secretariat Service (CSS). Those holding technical posts considered themselves to be more prestigious than CSS officials. That reminds me of an interesting case of my superintendent, R.K. Chatterjee, who preferred to switch over and strove hard to be appointed as an assistant information officer on a slightly lower pay scale. The highest post in the general category was that of administrative officer, then held by Rai Sahib C.N. Sen, a highly polished and pleasant gentleman. The gazetted posts in the Imperial Secretariat Service (ISS) were those of superintendents and assistant secretaries. The former, with a good record, were usually bestowed with titles of Rai Sahib or Khan Sahib and the latter with those of Rai Bahadur or Khan Bahadur.

By the time I came to Delhi, the war had extended to South-East Asia, with India emerging as a major centre of operation and an important part of the China-Burma-India theatre. Over 1,00,000 American troops were now stationed in India. They had set up the US Office of War Information at Delhi, which liaised with the Press Information Bureau. The American war establishment in India gave employment to numerous Indians and by September 1944, their number had risen to 79,000. There were also quite a few American journalists in India and according to the British War Office records, secret measures were taken to keep them under surveillance. The Government of India was irked by the Americans' informal and friendly encounters with Indians and their criticism of the British administration in India.

The mounting war expenditure led to economy measures in every possible field of government activity. The long-established practice of the government moving to the summer capital of Simla for a six-month period was suspended. There was a phenomenal demand for various goods for consumption by the military, resulting in shortages for the civilian population. This led to rationing and price control. A new-rich class emerged in the guise of army contractors who contributed generously to the war fund. Some of them were rewarded with the titles of Rai Sahib and Rai Bahadur, then symbols of social status and prestige. Around this time, I met someone who claimed to be a contractor for supplying stationery items to government offices to meet the shortage of imported products. I was amused to find that he was supplying packets of thorns to serve as steel pins, thereby saving steel for the war. He had engaged a number of labourers who picked up thorns from the cluster of bushes spread all over the ridge in Delhi. He would then get them packed in small paper pouches, each containing 100 pieces. Handy staplers were unknown and it was such fun using thorns to pin office papers.

The war period also witnessed a notable increase in the prices of all food products and consumer goods. There were significant signs of galloping inflation, which economists attributed to the vast increase in circulation of the rupee. The Indian government provided rupee funds to finance the British war expenditure and in turn was credited with an equivalent amount in sterling. Prof. C.N. Vakil, an eminent economist, at that time came out with his famous book *The Falling Rupee*. To alleviate the hardship faced by government employees, it was decided to grant 'dearness allowance' with salary. Further, in view of an acute shortage of government accommodation, the staff was provided with house rent and conveyance allowances. Two fair price shops were also opened, one in North Block and another near Gole Dak Khana, exclusively for government employees. They could buy some food and consumer items, mostly imported for specified amounts, fixed according to their emoluments.

I would like to recall the ambience of North Block in those days of the Raj. Everything was spick and span and the corridors were covered with coir matting to avoid noise of shoe steps. The liveried peons wearing belts with shining brass buckles could be seen carrying files and talking in whispers if they encountered any colleague on the way. The food canteens then run by private contractors deserve a mention here. It was amusing to find one Hindu canteen and the other a Muslim one, both on the second floor dominated by the secretariat staff. All senior officers occupied rooms on the first floor, where the executive councillors had their magnificent palatial chambers. For officers, there was a splendid eating place on the first floor run by Sanobar Khan, who maintained a troupe of liveried waiters and served only European dishes for lunch. Tea and snacks were usually served to officers in their rooms. I still remember Khan's delicious dishes and skilfully prepared Darjeeling tea, full of aroma and served in English crockery.

There was an unprecedented expansion of government departments during the war and a number of hutment blocks were built to provide office accommodation. The attached and subordinate offices of the main departments were mostly shifted from the North and South Blocks to these temporary structures. The PIB being an attached office was moved to 'N' Block, now replaced by the Rail Bhavan. Though built for wartime needs, a few of these hutments still survive and serve as office space even after almost seventy years. Moving out of North Block was not a pleasant experience as we were deprived of the then operating air conditioning comfort. The equipment installed for this purpose was still in working order and every room was furnished with a blower duct which delivered air according to the season. At the hutments, the PWD (Public Works Department) installed 'khus tattis' during summer and supplied electric heaters in winter. With the passage of time, desert coolers and air conditioners appeared on the scene. It is interesting to point out that these were provided to officers according to their rank and salary while the staff had to make do with fans.

World War II ended in May 1945 with the victory of Allied powers over Germany followed by the surrender of Japan in August. In order to provide employment to the demobilized military personnel, a Directorate General of Resettlement and Employment was set up under the labour department. As my appointment was temporary, I was keen to join one of the Central services on a regular basis. Therefore, I sat for the Central Services Competitive Examination in September 1945. Having qualified with a high score in the written examination, I was called by the Federal Public Service Commission for an interview in December 1945. The selection board grilled me for more than fifteen minutes and disqualified me by granting only 100 marks out of 300, just five marks short of the mandatory 105. I would have been on the selected list but for this unfair requirement, which later came up for much criticism and was abolished. Looking back, I now feel that it was a blessing in disguise since I was fated to be a technocrat and an international trade expert, spending a good part of my working life in foreign lands and not ending up as a bureaucrat in some provincial capital.

The Press Information Bureau, which witnessed notable expansion during the war, continued to flourish with its increased strength thanks to major political developments relating to the ensuing transfer of power to Indians. In those days the print media had no access to senior officers and policymakers in government departments. Press correspondents had to rely on the information officers concerned who doled out news to them. I recall how a team of officials set up a camp office at Simla during the historic conference there in 1945 when the British government held negotiations with the Indian political parties led by the Congress and Muslim League leaders: Maulana Azad, Jawaharlal Nehru, and M.A. Jinnah. The PIB team had to work overtime to cover the day-to-day developments and feed the press. Its photo section was equally active and provided photographs of leaders going in rickshaws on the Mall with crowds of spectators watching them. Nehru choosing to ride a horse and not take a rickshaw made for a news item. The Simla Conference was followed by the historic Cabinet Mission in early 1946, which again enhanced the PIB's importance.

As for me, this stint in PIB was quite valuable as it enabled me to learn a great deal about the functioning of different government departments and the role of bureaucracy under British masters. They had established a machinery of governance with comprehensive rules and regulations that earned the title of a 'steel frame'. In fact, my two-year experience in the PIB proved to be valuable throughout my long career in the government and the United Nations.

Among my senior colleagues in the PIB still etched in my memory, the ones who extended guidance and help in my assigned tasks were R.C. Asthana, Mahabir Sahai, K.K. Nair (Chaitanya, the famous scholar-author), Balraj Bowry and R.K. Chatterjee. It is relevant to point out that unlike bureaucrats, there was a professional fellow feeling amongst us holding technical posts and we met one another on equal terms. After retirement when I turned a freelance writer, the late K.K. Nair encouraged and guided me in my research during the 1990s for my sumptuously illustrated book *Nautch Girls of India* published in 1996. Besides, the late B.R. Bowry, editorial consultant with Allied Publishers, helped me in the publication of my first book *Lahore: A Sentimental Journey* in 1993. Another colleague, Raj Kakar, who left PIB and joined *Hindustan Times*, became a lifelong friend who inspired and assisted me throughout my writing career until his passing away in 1995. Then I remember my colleague and classmate from Government College, Lahore, the late Amanullah Sardar, who retired as the principal information officer of the Pakistan government. Another jovial character was Syyed Jafri, the Urdu journalist, who is better known as a poet and was a master of humour and satire. During the 1950s he came to Delhi to participate in the Indo-Pakistan mushairas. I remember his dig at the politicians of the subcontinent for their lack of substance and knowledge: '*Wo zamin ki poochhte hain, asman kehta hun main*! *Jab samajh mein kuchh nahin aata toh han kehta hun main*' (When they ask me about earthly matters I speak of heavenly affairs; when I don't comprehend anything I merely nod 'yes'). Another amusing hit by him was on the United Nations, i.e., 'USA *ka* U *hai baqi* no *hi* no' (The letter 'U' stands for the USA, and 'N' and 'O' imply no one else).

How true is the old saying that in our ripe old age it is easier to recall events that occurred fifty to sixty years ago than those of the recent past. It is like watching a beautiful landscape from a hilltop as it extends to the horizon but failing to note the flowery shrubs and plants on the slope below us.

4

Glimpses of Imperial New Delhi – 1940s

NEW DELHI, THE IMPERIAL CAPITAL, WAS officially inaugurated in February 1931 by the viceroy, Lord Irwin. He celebrated the occasion with a grand banquet attended by the high-ranking British ruling elite who dined off gold plates. Much has been written about the planned layout of the city, its magnificent buildings designed by Lutyens and Baker and the vast green Bungalow Zone. No historian or chronicler has however recorded anything significant about the Indian segment of Lutyens's New Delhi, the Delhi Imperial Zone (DIZ) area, which was the residential hub of the Indian staff of the Imperial Secretariat. Nestling under neat foliage it was a pure garden city, a city within the city of New Delhi. It had nothing oriental about it. Unlike any other Indian city marked by its variety of dwellings, bazaars and streets, here the dominant feature was uniformity.

I landed here in July 1944 and was captivated by the delightful ambience of this New Delhi. This mini-city in the DIZ area was bounded by Reading Road (Mandir Marg) on the west, Irwin Road

(Baba Kharak Singh Marg) on the east, Panchkuian Road on the north and Park Street on the south. The well-designed residential quarters were grouped in squares named after prominent imperial figures including former viceroys and governors such as Clive, Cornwallis, Hastings, Dalhousie, Lawrence, Nicholson, Lumsden and others. The most prominent block with extensive lawns was the Havelock Square close to Gole Dak Khana on Havelock Road (Kali Bari Marg), which extended up to Reading Road. The roads bifurcated the squares. Planned in a hierarchical manner, the staff quarters were classified in five categories, i.e. A, B, C, D and E – the last intended for lower division clerks (LDCs) with a starting pay of Rs 60 per month, and the others too were strictly according to salary. A striking feature of staff quarters in different squares was the provision of spacious lawns in front, extending up to the roads. The back doors of the quarters opened into service lanes frequented by vendors licensed by the New Delhi Municipal Committee (NDMC). Some residents crazy about pure and fresh milk kept their own cows, which were lodged in PWD cowsheds located in the vicinity. It is interesting to note that the staff quarters were further classified into 'Orthodox' and 'Unorthodox' types, the latter intended for Anglo-Indians and other Indians with a modern way of life. These were equipped with Western-style toilets and provided with an exclusive lawn in front instead of enclosed courtyards of the orthodox types. The bachelor staff were allotted 'chummeries', again of orthodox and unorthodox types, located near the Gole Market and Gole Dak Khana. The address of the allotted residence faithfully reflected the rank, seniority and pay scale of the occupant. Before World War II, the highest post held by an Indian was that of an assistant secretary in a government department or an officer supervisor at the Army General Headquarters. The incumbents were usually bestowed the titles of Rai Bahadur, Khan Bahadur and Sardar Bahadur, and mostly allotted bungalows on Talkatora Road and Queen Mary Avenue (Pandit Pant Marg). Next below were the superintendents in departments who earned the titles of Rai Sahibs and occupied 'A' type quarters or smaller bungalows on Allenby Road (Dr Bishambar Das Marg). The exteriors of all quarters and bungalows were spick and span as these were cleaned and whitewashed by the PWD every year. So were the roads in New Delhi, which were cleaned and sprinkled with water every day. During summer, each quarter was fitted with khus tatties to keep the indoors cool with pleasant-smelling air, duly wetted by the PWD's mashqi (water-carrier) who carried water in a of goatskin mashk.

A major landmark of the DIZ area was the Gole Market. There was a chain of shops from provision to cloth stores which catered to the needs of the government staff living at walking distance in the surrounding residential complex. The octagonal market containing meat, poultry, and vegetable and fruit shops formed a significant part in the axis planned by Lutyens as part of New Delhi's layout. Close by was Doctors Lane, where the famous Dr Ghosh had his clinic. Another eminent doctor nearby was the child specialist K.L. Jain. The adjoining Baird Road (Bangla Sahib Marg) was flanked by a few shops on both sides. There was then the popular Union Restaurant, which provided regular meals on a monthly basis, a boon for the bachelor staff who would cycle down there during lunch hour and have their dinner before going home. I too availed this facility for a few months. For only thirty-five rupees a month, one could have two meals with a bowl of dal, a plate of seasonal vegetables and chapattis without count. I recall some health-conscious Punjabis kept their own stock of pure ghee to enrich their diet. The restaurant also offered credit facilities to customers, who were mostly government employees and their official identity card was adequate security for payment.

Other landmarks of this mini-city were Kali Bari, the Bengali centre for religious and cultural activities; the Lakshmi Narayan temple, commonly known as Birla temple; and the ancient Hanuman temple on Irwin Road where every Tuesday a regular mela was held. A large number of vendors from Old Delhi assembled there to sell their wares. Perched on the ground with gas lamps displaying their wares and musical clamouring to attract customers, they presented a delightful sight. The Birla temple with its vast complex attracted both worshippers and idlers. During the 1940s it had become a popular meeting place for both old and young, with the temple backyard overlooking the ridge offering a picturesque view of the sunset.

The leading commercial centre of New Delhi was the majestic Connaught Place (CP). I was impressed by its circular grandeur, sparkling white columns supporting palatial buildings, with lordly shops opening out to its spacious verandahs. Baptized in alphabetical order, each block prided on having its own famous shops and stores. I vividly remember the sights and sounds of this august place, a popular meeting ground during the 1940s. CP's 'A' Block housed the grand store Hamilton & Co., dealing in diamonds, gems and jewels and catering to high-ranking officials and Indian princes. Some other leading shops were Enid, ladies dress makers; Kinsey Brothers, photographers; Phelps & Co., civil and military drapers and outfitters; Trevelyan & Clarke; Chinese Art Palace; Empire Stores; Edward Keventer; S.C. Sharma & Co., drapers and tailors; Oriental Carpets; Uberoi Sports; B. Lilaram & Co.; Sahib Singh Chemists; Kemp & Co.; and Ivory Palace. The Regal building housed the famous Army & Navy Stores, while Queensway (Janpath) was the site of Ranken & Co., Cooke & Kelvey, silverware and watch merchants; and the famous hairdresser A.N. John for sahibs and memsahibs.

Also located in CP were the four cinema houses, viz. Odeon, Plaza, Regal, and Rivoli which screened only English movies. The leading restaurants were Devicos, Wenger's and Piccadily with fancy ballrooms. These served only European dishes and foreign liquor. There were no pubs but the cinemas had licensed bars for ticket holders. In practice they served other clients as well, a wartime relaxation. The sahibs were particular in banning Indian cuisine in CP's Inner Circle as the smell of Indian curries was supposed to pollute the refreshing atmosphere of the place. It was only in the Outer Circle that a concession was granted to Luxmi Restaurant and Madras Hotel, which served Indian food. During the war, Nirulas in the Outer Circle also joined this group.

The Middle Circle of Connaught Place with very few shops was more or less a service road. No construction was permitted there and backyards of buildings in the Inner and Outer Circles hedged the road. There were a few well-maintained public toilets with attendants to take care of their cleanliness. There were also a couple of motor service garages. Cars were so few that they were usually parked in front of the shops in the Inner Circle, right in the middle of the road, with traffic freely moving on both sides. In fact, the road was bifurcated by street-lighting poles, the kind which still line Kingsway (Rajpath) from Great Place (Vijay Chowk) to the War Memorial (India Gate).

During the war years, with the declining number of sahibs and memsahibs, leading British stores catering to their needs faced a noticeable slump in their business. The restaurants, however, did roaring business with new Indian clientele. It became fashionable to flock to Wenger's and Devicos for a cup of tea and snacks after office hours. There used to be live bands for tea dances on wooden floors. The cinema houses also attracted crowds since a new generation of westernized Indian civil and military officials preferred to watch English movies.

A few doctors and homeopaths had their clinics in the Outer Circle. There was also a billiards parlour, the game being very much in fashion with the youth. Buses also plied on the Outer

Circle road. There was then a trolleybus terminus at the meeting point of Chelmsford Road. The solitary trolleybus ran from the Outer Circle to Tis Hazari with stops at New Delhi Railway Station, Ram Nagar and Qutab Road, linking Old Delhi, Civil Lines to New Delhi.

New Delhi was then a garden city with green patches covering greater area than the buildings. The constant watering of the lawns of Lutyens's bungalows and those on the Central Vista as well as vast green spaces including Lady Willingdon (Lodhi) and Talkatora Gardens kept the underground water level quite high. This was also cited as a reason for not permitting construction beyond two floors in New Delhi. The ridge area on the west of Reading Road was a vast hilly track with wild growth. Sahibs climbing up from Lovers Lane (Mandir Lane) went riding on Ridge Road, which had a horse-riding track.

Panchkuian Road was a broad avenue with railway officers' bungalows lining up on the right from Outer Circle up to the crossing of Baird Road. On the opposite side stood the famous Lady Hardinge Medical College. Further on the right were double-storey blocks with shops of furniture, sanitary fittings, hardware, etc., with residential flats on the first floor. At the end of the road stood the walled cremation ground. This was the western limit of New Delhi, from where a road over the elevated ridge branched off to Pusa Road on the left and Arya Samaj Road leading to the Karol Bagh area.

Until World War II, practically every staff member was provided with government accommodation. The war years witnessed an enormous expansion of government staff with the emergence of new departments and offices, and the great proliferation in the scope and volume of government activity. India had become a vital source of men and materials for the war effort. This led to an acute shortage of both office space and living accommodation.

Temporary structures called hutments were built in the vicinity of North and South Blocks for offices and elsewhere for housing the staff. But when demand outstripped the supply, officers were even lodged in tented accommodation in the vast open spaces near Hardinge (Tilak) Bridge. The government also resorted to requisitioning some privately owned houses and apartments to accommodate officials. The war years led to more than doubling of New Delhi's population. In spite of large-scale construction of buildings in new areas and wartime structures, New Delhi had more than adequate infrastructure. There was twenty-four-hour water supply and no power cuts. Later, in 1944 there were restrictions on new electricity connections but no shortage of water.

When I landed in New Delhi in 1944, I stayed temporarily with some relations in Havelock Square. It was quite an ordeal to find a place to live in the capital. I tried to seek help from the Capital Estate Agency in Connaught Place, the solitary firm in this business, but to no avail. House owners welcomed only married tenants and even government servants hesitated to share their quarters with bachelors. The YMCA (Young Men's Christian Association) hostel offered accommodation to bachelors but it had a long waiting list. It was after considerable effort and recommendations that I got a room with a family in the Western Extension Area (WEA) of Pusa Road, where a number of newly constructed houses had been requisitioned by the government for their staff.

There were no taxis or autorickshaws, and the chief mode of transport was the tonga, which plied all over New Delhi. Tongas made regular trips to the secretariat from Gole Market, Gole Dak Khana and even from Ajmeri Gate via Connaught Place. There was a private bus service run by Gwalior Northern India Transport Company, which had expanded its operations to facilitate transport to the secretariat from some additional sites. While the younger lot chose to cycle down to the North or South Block, the principal destination for office goers, the older generation preferred to go by tonga. In fact it was a common practice with them to have a group of four and engage a tonga on a monthly sharing basis, which would pick them up from their respective quarters in the morning and bring them back after office hours. The office peak hours in the morning presented a delightful sight of a row of racing tongas and a procession of cyclists riding in the middle of the road, with few cars on the scene.

Coming to social life, there were 'clubs', essentially a British tradition. The Imperial Delhi Gymkhana Club was originally an exclusive meeting place of British civilian and military officers but during the Second World War, some senior Indian officers were given club membership. The word 'Gymkhana' is derived from the Hindustani word 'gaindkhana' meaning ball or racquet court. There was Chelmsford Club for Indian officers, eminent professionals, and civilians. For the secretariat staff there was Talkatora Club, now named Central Secretariat Club. My popular meeting place with friends and colleagues was either the India Coffee House on Queensway or the United Coffee House in Connaught Place. Occasionally we went to Kashmere Gate to meet friends from Old Delhi and watch Indian movies. It was the leading commercial hub before the birth of New Delhi. YMCA near Gole Dak Khana was another meeting place for indoor games as well as for sports such as tennis and badminton.

The older turbaned generation of officials would usually socialize in the evening with neighbours in the 'Square' lawns. Sitting on cots and collapsible chairs, they could be heard discussing politics or indulging in office gossip. The womenfolk usually stayed inside and had their meetings in the courtyards.

There was little contact with the opposite sex especially for newcomers to the imperial capital. There was then practically no female staff in government offices. There were some Anglo-Indian and Christian girls working in the telephone and telegraph offices and in the Women Auxiliary Corps who would date the British soldiers. A novel sight at this time was that of American soldiers. With emoluments and perks far higher than the BORs (British Other Ranks), they managed to woo these girls away from them and could be seen entertaining them in fashionable hotels, restaurants and bars.

It is interesting to note that while planning New Delhi, the British did not earmark any red-light area, which was an essential part of every Indian city and cantonment. The oldest profession continued to thrive during the Raj. There were well-staffed brothels in Bombay, Calcutta and other main cities and cantonments visited by British civilians and soldiers. The missionaries had protested but the official view was that prostitution fulfilled a socially necessary function, and banning it might lead to offences such as criminal assault and rape. Coming to Delhi, the traditional red-light area in Chawri Bazaar was shifted in 1940 to G.B. Road, outside Ajmeri Gate, not far from Thomson Road. Perhaps the British authorities thought its location would meet the demands of both Old and New Delhi. I recall in 1944 there were accomplished and talented singing girls like Gulab Bai, Raj Kanwar, Mushtari Bai, Maya and Vidya, who entertained visitors in their salons on G.B. Road. Incidentally, I learnt that Maya and Vidya used to move to Simla during summer months along with the exodus of the government to its summer capital. Evidently, some colourful officials must have been their regular patrons. There were also brothels on G.B. Road with sex workers to answer the needs of their clients. We never heard of any police raids to catch the sex trade operators in any other part of the city, and the modern call-girl profession was still decades away.

5

Publications, Commerce Ministry

THE COMMERCE DEPARTMENT IN EARLY 1946 set up the Commercial Publications Branch headed by S.R.S. Raghavan, a senior PIB officer and former editor of *Commerce*, then a leading Indian weekly. Raghavan preferred to be designated as editor of the new unit, instead of the customary title of 'director' which was assumed a decade later. His team comprised subeditors and commercial investigators. I joined as an investigator but within a year I was promoted to subeditor/assistant director, a Class I post which I held for nearly a decade.

The commerce department then dealt with foreign trade, company law, insurance, plantation industries, customs tariffs and shipping. The Government of India's trade missions abroad headed by trade commissioners functioned under the commerce department. The CP branch handled commercial publicity and through its publications kept the media as well as the Chambers of Commerce and Trade Associations duly informed about the ongoing trends in India's foreign trade and government policy announcements concerning trade and economy.

We produced three publications: *Indian Market Review* and *Foreign Market Review*, both weeklies, and *Indian Trade Bulletin*, a fortnightly which was under my charge. The bulletin carried feature articles on Indian trade and industry and comprehensive information on government policy notifications and also the prospects of expanding trade in new markets and the scope of exporting new products. There were then four economic and commercial journals, *Eastern Economist*, *The Capital*, *Commerce* and *Indian Finance*. I had to carefully study their comments and views on government policy announcements and notifications. The two weeklies, *Indian Market Review* and *Foreign Market Review*, were distributed free to the media and Chambers of Commerce but the *Indian Trade Bulletin* was priced at eight annas (half a rupee) a copy. It was printed by I.M.H. Press in Chandni Chowk, Delhi, entrusted with the job by the controller of printing and stationery, Government of India.

I recall that before going to the press, manuscripts of the bulletin contents were approved by the joint secretary (commerce), then A.S. Lall, ICS. He had instructed me to bring the manuscripts to him after 5 p.m., when he glanced through the entire text, giving his remarks on contents and even suggestions. In 1951, the Ministry of Industry was merged with commerce, resulting in the creation of a new Ministry of Commerce and Industry. A.S. Lall, who took keen interest in our publications, called me up and gave instructions to convert the fortnightly trade bulletin into a monthly named *Journal of Industry & Trade*. In fact, he took a piece of paper and designed the title cover, suggesting blue lettering. It now covered a much wider field and soon emerged as the leading official periodical, a mouthpiece of government activities and policy announcements on trade and industry. Among new features introduced in the journal were regular write-ups covering the monthly reports sent by India's trade representatives in our missions abroad. When Parliament was in session, the information of economic and commercial interest provided during the 'Question Hour' was also included. Further, the state governments were asked to send us all the relevant information about economic developments in the state and related official activities. This was included in the journal's new section, 'News from the States'.

Another important publication of the ministry was the *Indian Trade Journal* issued by the Directorate of Commercial Intelligence and Statistics located in Calcutta. After Independence, it was decided to transfer it to our publications branch, and an OSD (officer on special duty), P.K. Panikkar, was appointed to handle its publication from Delhi. This journal carried monthly foreign trade statistics and more importantly all tender notices issued by government departments. Calcutta was then hailed as the commercial capital and all major industrial and commercial business houses, especially those owned by the British, had their headquarters there. The Associated Chamber of Commerce was also located in Calcutta. Traditionally, its annual session used to be addressed by the viceroy, who made important policy announcements on this occasion. There was a powerful business lobby in Calcutta whose views and opinions were duly considered by the commerce ministry. They posed stiff opposition to the government's decision to transfer the *Indian Trade Journal* to Delhi. Eventually the decision was reversed and Panikkar was appointed as director of exhibitions in the ministry.

Around 1950, the defence ministry set up its School of Foreign Languages for government officials. It started with teaching French, German and Russian. The classes were held at 8.30 a.m., before office hours. The preliminary course took one year and the advanced took two. I got myself sponsored by the ministry and successfully completed the two-year course in French. I still remember the French teacher, Madame Ehsanulla, a well-known

French lady from Lahore, who taught in Forman Christian College there. The French language diploma proved to be a boon for me when I joined the foreign service a few years later, where it was obligatory to pass an examination in one foreign language.

Returning to the *Journal of Industry and Trade*, the controller of printing and stationery decided in 1952 to transfer its printing from a private press in Delhi to the Government of India Press, Simla, which had some idle capacity. By then, the journal had become quite popular among business circles, with thousands of subscribers. This inspired me to propose inclusion of advertisements in the journal from the Indian trade and industry, a clear departure from the established government policy. Initially it was rejected by the senior ministry officials. However, I did not lose hope and kept pursuing my proposal by indicating the revenue element and also its utility for trade promotion. As it was the only official commercial publication distributed abroad through our missions, I highlighted the fact that advertisements of Indian products would inform the foreign buyers about prospects of importing these products from India. Finally, I was able to convince K.B. Lal, joint secretary (commerce), who was then a leading policymaker, and my proposal was approved. Within a short period, there was a flood of advertisements and an increase in circulation. I enjoyed the increased volume of work and regular visits to Simla, where I went to examine the dummy and supervise the timely production of the journal.

Simla in the early 1950s was a delightful place still retaining some of the ambience and flavour of the imperial days. Government officials on tour would stay at the Grand Hotel managed by the Estate Office. The tariff for a comfortable single room with attached bath was only Rs 4/- per day if on duty and Rs 6/- for private visits. Then the maximum daily allowance for officers was fixed at Rs 10/-. The catering was done by a contractor at prescribed rates for different meals. There was also a provision for hiring a kitchenette with one's own cook when staying for a longer duration. I used to avail this facility and lodge my family here during the summer months of May and June. Simla was still the most popular summer resort for Delhi bureaucrats and one would see familiar faces on the Mall in the evenings. According to old government rules, an officer on tour used to get an extra rail fare for incidental expenses. This came to about Rs 40/-, the cost of a Scotch bottle. This sojourn at Simla was not only a pleasant diversion from the Delhi office routine but also a boon for physical fitness as daily visits to the government press made me walk more than six miles.

Another interesting aspect of the Simla visits was an opportunity of socializing with my old Lahore friends who had settled there after Partition. The East Punjab government was now established at Simla while the new capital Chandigarh was under construction. Earlier, Simla used to be the summer capital of Punjab, and the governor and his secretariat had their establishment at Chhota Simla away from the Mall and the Central government offices. Many wealthy Punjabi families owned and maintained their houses at Simla. The pleasant Simla trips continued for over three years until I was posted abroad and bade farewell to the commercial publications branch of the ministry.

While I was stuck to the same post for over eight years, my fellow economists had in the meantime attained better positions in the expanding Planning Commission and some new economic wings of other ministries. So I applied for the post of deputy director (public relations) in the Indian Standards Institution (ISI), a semi-government body under the commerce ministry. I appeared for an interview before a high-powered selection board chaired by Commerce Secretary H.V.R. Iyengar with Sir Shri Ram, a leading industrialist of the time, the chairman of ISI and two other board members. This turned out to be a consequential event in my official career. I had studied the activities of the ISI and was able to answer questions put to me and make suggestions for expanding the ISI membership through dissemination of information about its benefits to the industry. Anyway, though I impressed the selection board, it decided to appoint one Mr Bhatia who was already officiating in the post. However, the commerce secretary recorded a note that paved the way for a new chapter in my career. The text of the note dated 9 September 1955 given below shows the fair-mindedness and assessment of merit by an eminent personality like H.V.R. Iyengar, whom I had never met before.

> Mr Nevile has personality and pleasant manners as well as intelligence. After the orders regarding Mr Bhatia have been approved, I would like Mr Nevile informed of the very favourable impression he created on the Committee. An extract may be kept on his personal record.

Soon after this episode, I was asked to apply for the post of deputy director of exhibitions in the ministry. My case was strongly recommended by the director of exhibitions, Mr P.K. Panikkar, who had known me since 1946 when he was OSD in the commercial publications. My appointment was approved by the secretary, H.V.R. Iyengar; Mr Panikkar even congratulated and told me to join at the earliest before his proceeding on tour abroad. The final appointment order required the commerce minister's signature on the file, a mere formality in those days. Surprisingly, the then minister, T.T. Krishnamachari, ordered the appointment of one Brij Bhushan from the Lok Sabha Secretariat as deputy director of exhibitions. Panikkar told me that some political influence had played its part and I was therefore left out. Shortly thereafter, I was offered the post of second secretary (commercial) in our embassy in Tokyo.

Until 1955, it was the prerogative of the commerce ministry to appoint their own officers and staff in the commercial wings of our missions abroad. The Ministry of External Affairs then decided to integrate all commercial posts within the Indian Foreign Service (IFS) cadre. The Foreign Service Board, with the commerce secretary as member, selected officers for posting in missions abroad. I was selected as second secretary (commercial) thanks to Iyengar, who gave weightage to my experience and prevailed upon the Foreign Service Board to approve my appointment. I was the last non-IFS person to be posted as a commercial officer abroad. In the meantime, the Indian Economic Service (IES) had been constituted and I was encadred service with 1948 seniority.

Before my departure for Tokyo, I called on Iyengar to express my gratitude and seek his blessings. He smilingly said,'You deserve it and I have spoken to Ambassador B.R. Sen about you.' I also called on Joint Secretary K.B. Lal for a full briefing about my new assignment. An institution in himself and principal architect of India's foreign trade policy, Mr Lall was also the founding father of 'Rupee Trade'. He was the brain behind the annual 'Red Book' containing the rules and regulations governing the issue of import–export licences. It was said to have been designated 'Red' after his name. He informed me about the current trends of Indo-Japanese trade and instructed me on how to deal with the Japanese officials and businessmen. This was the beginning of my lifelong association with him as his dedicated disciple.

Finally, I would like to say something about my colleagues during my decade-long spell in commercial publications. My chief, S.R.S. Raghavan, was a noble person who treated me like a son. He even arranged a small reception when I got married in 1947 and made every member of the editorial staff contribute for a wedding present. Among my colleagues, I fondly remember M.M. Taqi, who introduced me to his friend – the renowned poet

Faiz Ahmad Faiz – then a colonel in the Indian Army. Then there were V. Ramakrishnan Rao, a learned economist; Mr Narasimhan, a financial journalist and Sanskrit scholar who amused us during lunch hour with erotic tales from the epics; and Raj K. Nigam, who became a lifelong friend till he passed away in 2001. After a couple of years in commercial publications, he went for a PhD to the London School of Economics. He had a distinguished career in the Indian Economic Service (IES), and later became an eminent author of several books on India's public sector.

6

Elopement and Civil Marriage

UNTIL EARLY 1940S, THERE WAS PRACTICALLY no interaction between young boys and girls. Co-education was still a topic of debate among college students. The old custom of early marriage was now frowned upon and the prospective bridegroom was expected to have a regular source of income, especially in urban Punjab. An arranged marriage was the accepted norm. There were no marriage bureaux or agencies and it was left to family friends and relations to handle marriage proposals. An innovation that crept into vogue was the formal meeting of two families, with the boy being given an opportunity to see the girl, usually over a cup of tea. The girl's consent was invariably taken for granted and the marriage deal was struck after the boy gave a nod. Elaborate engagement and marriage ceremonies followed. The groom, adorned in a wedding costume and crowned turban, riding a horse and even carrying a sword, would march with a baraat led by a uniformed brass band towards the bride's abode. Another set of ceremonies there and the bride would be packed off in a doli. As I grew up watching these rituals, I developed abhorrence for this ostentatious tamasha and meaningless jubilation. Another undesirable feature was the dowry custom. It was customary to provide the groom with full attire from head to toe and also a wrist watch. A close relation of the girl's side was usually entrusted with the task of taking the groom out for shopping and buying everything of his choice. Sometimes a branded bicycle was also added to the shopping list. It was common knowledge that shopkeepers were hinted in advance about the girl side's budget. I had been a witness to this exercise and was disgusted with the entire dowry system.

By the 1940s, Indian cinema had emerged as a major influence on the social scene. Apart from classical love legends like *Laila Majnu*, *Shirin Farhad* and *Heer Ranjha*. Other popular films like *Chandidas*, *Devdas*, *Achhut Kanya*, *Kangan* and *Bandhan*, etc., were all love stories. Then we had Hollywood movies soaked in romance and love scenes. My generation, now on the threshold of youth, began craving feminine company. But there was a lurking fear that this pursuit would disrupt concentration on studies and adversely affect future career prospects. Besides, it was important to secure a well-paid job before stepping into the marriage market. Sometimes one's academic achievements would bring matrimonial offers from far-sighted parents. I recall receiving an engagement offer when I won a matriculation scholarship, standing third in Punjab. Fortunately, my father declined.

It was after attaining the BA (Hons) top position in college that I felt inclined towards pursuing friendships with the opposite sex. I recall a young girl of my neighbourhood who persuaded my mother to ask me to help her in studies for her matric exam. I soon found out that she was hopeless in studies and more interested in being alone with me and enjoy dalliance. She would clasp my hands and exchange passionate glances. One day my father opened the door of my room and saw her sitting close to me. That was the end of both coaching and flirting but without any hard feelings. On my part, I was glad to have learnt my first lessons in the love game. The art of physically attracting the opposite sex needs careful study to ensure one does not err and cause any offence. Thus, any deliberate brushing with the female body must seem unintentional and accidental, to be ignored. A couple of other parties with average looks came my way and I felt some thrill in practising this art. Falling in love and pining for the object of one's adulation was still something alien to me. My foremost objective was to get through the Central services competition and join government officialdom. But destiny had other plans.

In July 1941, my uncle (husband of my father's first cousin) came with his family to Lahore for my brother's marriage. I was glad to meet my cousins, especially Savitri, now an attractive sixteen-year-old girl. I had visited Delhi a couple of times earlier and stayed with them but had treated her as a little girl. She had done her matric in first division a year earlier but my old-fashioned conservative uncle did not send her to college. He was more concerned with her marriage and dowry. Instead of sitting idle, Savitri pursued studies and passed the highest Hindi examination. Savitri's elder sister, Pritam, had been married off when she was seventeen and was living in Lahore. Her husband M.L. Bhardwaj, also our relation, was a journalist working with the *Civil and Military Gazette* (CMG) newspaper. I liked Savitri's great interest in further studies and encouraged her to do so privately. Her brother, who was two years older, after failing once, did his matric along with her and was sent to college. She was unhappy over this discrimination by her parents and confided in me her desire to become a teacher. She had requested Pritam to persuade their father for her admission to college but to no avail. My uncle's family stayed with us for a month and Savitri and I had ample time to develop a fondness for each other within the limits of our relationship. Moreover, I became a guide and supporter to her further pursuit of studies.

In January 1942, I was returning from Bombay where I had gone with my university group. I broke my journey at Delhi ostensibly to see my uncle's family, but in reality for meeting Savitri. She had joined a private coaching college to continue her studies. Later, in April, she came to Lahore to sit for the FA (formative assessment) examination. She came with my aunt and spent a week with us. She would have stayed longer but her sister had moved to Delhi with her husband, who had been appointed as information officer with the Government of India.

With our interrelationships, we were quite close to the Bhardwaj family living in our neighbourhood at Nisbet Road. I was quite friendly with M.L. Bhardwaj's younger brothers: Mohni, of my age group and Chaman Lal, who was a couple of years senior to me in Government College. Both of them moved to Delhi and joined their brother's family there. Chaman Lal, also a journalist having worked for some time with the *Tribune*, joined the army as public relations officer. It was now wartime and there were quite a few job opportunities in the expanding activities of the Indian government. Bhardwaj was extremely fond of me from when I was younger and asked me to come over to Delhi after appearing for my MA examination. So in May 1943 I went to Delhi and stayed with my uncle's family at their house in Havelock Square. For me it meant renewal of contact with Savitri. I was happy to note her obvious delight on my visit. Bhardwaj lived close by on Allenby Road near Gole Dak Khana and we had frequent family get-togethers at either place.

Savitri managed to have one-to-one meetings with me on the pretext of seeking my guidance for her studies. By now, she had grown up and become an attractive young girl. She did not resist my passionate moves to fondle her. Soon, I felt her response was quite encouraging, giving the impression that she eagerly welcomed my advances. It did not take long to graduate to embracing and kissing whenever there was an opportunity.

On my career front, Bhardwaj tried for me in All India Radio but without success. I also appeared for an interview for the civilian gazetted officers, a new cadre introduced by the defence department, but could not make it. After spending a couple of months in Delhi, I returned to Lahore.

Two months later Savitri visited Lahore with Pritam for Mohni's engagement. Later, she told me that it was just an excuse to meet me. After the function she stayed with us for a few days before returning to Delhi. As my siblings were away at Simla, Savitri and I had all the time to ourselves. We even went together to watch K.L. Saigal's *Tansen* at Nishat Cinema. We were having an affair under the guise of a friendship between cousins. Both of us became vocal and expressed our love for each other, casting away the semblance of a conventional cousin brother–sister relation. For me the major factor in man–woman love was physical attraction and the ultimate physical bond. The idea of platonic love was alien to me and contrary to our ancient philosophy and literature. Then followed an exchange of letters with coded sweet nothings; a token of mutual reassurance. In February 1944, I went to Delhi to attend Chaman Lal Bhardwaj's marriage. Then Savitri came to Lahore in April 1944 to sit for her BA examination. This frequency in our meetings kept up the intensity of our emotional attachment and saved us from running the risk of 'out of sight, out of mind'. She stayed with us for a month and we had ample time to enjoy each other's company and exchange our vows. A month later, M.L. Bhardwaj wrote to me suggesting I apply for a journalist's post in his office, the Press Information Bureau. I did so and came to Delhi for a written test and interview along with nearly fifty candidates. After a month or so, I received an appointment letter and joined duties in Delhi in July 1944. I stayed with my uncle for a few months before moving to a rented place near Pusa Road. Savitri was overjoyed to have me in Delhi and claimed that this was the outcome of her prayers. She was now studying for Montessori course diploma and had already started teaching in a girls' school located at Gole Market.

This ushered in a new chapter in my life. I would occasionally visit my uncle's house and meet everyone. I had little interaction with my conservative uncle but my aunt was affectionate and often enquired how I managed my meals. She would ask me to come over for lunch on Sundays and showed a good deal of concern for me – her cousin brother's son. Though first cousins, my father had no sister and she had no brother and they had, over the past three decades, nursed their ties as brother and sister. Occasionally, I also visited M.L. Bhardwaj's house on Allenby Road and they too treated me like a family member. Savitri was often present there.

Savitri was careful to keep our romantic relationship a secret from everyone in the family. We began meeting outside occasionally. Later, I encouraged her to come to my place. I was then staying in an independent room with a separate entrance, rented to me by a decent family from Lahore. The old lady, head of the family, treated me like a son and showed no interest in my visitors. We now started a new element in our affair with exchange of love letters. Savitri would return my letters after reading to prevent any leakage at her end. One day I dropped my wallet containing our two letters at Bhardwaj's house. It was picked up by Pritam, who took the letters and returned my wallet the next day. The great secret was finally out. She confronted Savitri, who confessed everything and told her that she wanted to marry me. Pritam promised to keep the secret and explore ways and means to persuade the two families. Soon after, M.L. Bhardwaj was transferred to Lahore as head of the PIB's office there. Pritam's family left Delhi, leaving everything in cold storage but not without making the affair known to our families. There was hard talk between Savitri and her father, who threatened he would never allow this unholy alliance. My father also had his apprehensions and rushed to my grandfather in our village for his advice on the matter. My grandfather laughed it out, dismissing my father with the story of Lord Krishna having married Rukmani, his first cousin. So my family left the decision on me and showed readiness to perform the marriage if Savitri's parents agreed. Pritam kept consoling Savitri, hoping she would prevail upon her father in due course to agree with the marriage proposal.

Days and months passed by but there was no hopeful indication. I recall once telling Savitri to carry on with our affair without formal wedlock. A live-in relationship was still several decades away on the horizon. She dismissed it outright, pointing out that it might work out for me but for her it would not be possible to live with her family under those tense and strained circumstances. I kept away from Savitri's house and she too felt suffocated. Her father assured he would never force a marriage on her with anyone, but she must sever all relations with me. In the meantime, she began visiting me more often than before and to drown our depression we began gratifying our suppressed sexual demands. In a way this emboldened Savitri to defy her father. In this regard she received full support from her mother. On my part, I had no interest in a ceremonial marriage and persuaded Savitri to go in for a civil marriage in court. I applied in a Delhi court and was told to appear one month later. I had a full one month to organize her elopement from her house along with her personal effects. She was still teaching in the school and would leave the house in the morning. She made bundles and packets of all her personal items – clothing, books, etc., – and would hand them over to me outside her school. This drill was repeated ten to fifteen times and finally on the day of reckoning, she left for school in the morning only to be picked up by me. I took her to my friend Raj Kakar's house, where I had kept all her things. She changed into a red silk saree, the only one I had bought for her, and rushed in a tonga to the Kashmere Gate court. Our marriage was solemnized on 25 January 1947 by F.H.D. Teal, the registrar of marriages, with my friends M.L. Chopra, B.N. Sharma and R.K. Kakar acting as witnesses. The same evening we left for Dehradun for our honeymoon. Savitri's long letter to her father justifying her elopement and marriage was delivered by a messenger after the train had steamed off from Delhi railway station.

A couple of weeks after our return from our honeymoon, my father landed in Delhi along with my sister-in-law and younger brother. He had already distributed wedding cards to all his near and dear ones at Lahore, announcing the celebration of 'Griha parvesh' (stepping into home) of the bride. It was difficult to bring a marriage party to Delhi in February 1947 owing to the turbulent political situation in Punjab. M.L. Bhardwaj came along to represent the bride's family along with Tek Chand, Savitri's brother. He organized a traditional ceremonial wedding with the priest, performing the rituals at his friend M.L. Chawla's house in Lodhi Estate on 24 February 1947. In this way I ended up marrying the same girl twice. The next day we left for Lahore. We were received by our family members and friends who had brought the famous Soni's brass band to the railway station for welcoming us. A procession of about twenty to twenty-five tongas, led by the bandmaster and his team playing popular film tunes, marched to our house on Nisbet Road. For me and my wife, it was an amusing experience to go through another set of rituals before we stepped into the house. The ladies were singing traditional Punjabi songs to welcome the bride. Our house was decorated with flowers and colourful lights.

Later in the evening, there was the usual garden tea party in a shamiana put up in a large open space, close to our house. Over 300 guests assembled there to congratulate and bless the newlyweds. Quite a few of my friends who were in the know of my civil marriage had a big laugh and mocked my second marriage. My parents were happy and displayed the gorgeous sarees and jewellery they were giving to the bride. My friend R.D. Chopra, who was a press photographer, posted one of his cameramen to cover the festivities.

The next day, some intimate friends celebrated my wedding, men only, at the famous Punjab Association Club, finishing it off with song at Tamancha Jan's kotha in Hira Mandi, the celebrated entertainment quarters of Lahore.

The show over, we were back to our one-room abode in Delhi. There was no honeymoon this time.

7

Witness to Partition

THE MOMENTOUS HAPPENINGS OF 1946 PAVED the way for Partition and the emergence of two independent states of India and Pakistan. In pursuance of their decision to transfer power to Indians, the British Labour government headed by Clement Attlee sent the Cabinet Mission in March 1946. After conducting extensive discussions and negotiations with the Congress and Muslim League, the Cabinet Mission in May 1946 presented their plan as a solution to the opposing demands of the two main political parties. The plan envisaged a Union of India dealing with foreign affairs, defence and communications and having the power to raise finances required for those three areas of government activity. All other subjects and residuary powers were to vest with the provinces, which would be free to form groups on specific terms and conditions. After protracted confabulations, the Cabinet Mission Plan was rejected by both political parties in July 1946. However, to the great disappointment of the Muslim League, Lord Wavell invited Jawaharlal Nehru to form an interim government, which he did on 16 August 1946.

The Muslim League announced 'Direct Action' to achieve their objective of Pakistan. This led to the 'Great Calcutta Killings' (the toll was about 5,000) which was a turning point in the history of Hindu–Muslim relations. Described as a civil war in miniature, it was followed by large-scale communal rioting in East Bengal, Bihar, UP and West Punjab. Apprehending repercussions in Delhi, curfew was imposed in some parts of Old Delhi, as too in Ajmal Khan Road in Karol Bagh. I recall how once returning home to Western Extension Area via Ajmal Khan Road market at night I was caught unawares by the police as curfew had been imposed there. I was detained at the police station along with others for questioning. The constables were rough and rude, threatening everyone with lock-up. I managed to meet the inspector and showed him my Government of India identity card. He politely took me to the backdoor of the station and let me off, telling me his name in case of an encounter with other policemen on the way. Later on, government officials were provided with curfew passes.

Lord Wavell, considering the volatile communal situation, accepted the Muslim League's demand of being recognized as the sole representative of Indian Muslims and invited the League in October 1946 to join the interim government.

The Congress and the League leaders in the cabinet could not see eye to eye on any question. Mutual suspicion and animosity wrecked the smooth working of the government. The ministers worked at cross purposes and the officialdom was polarized. The communal spirit affected the services. Muslim officials supported the Muslim League leaders and the Hindus sided with the Congress. What made matters worse was finance minister Liaqat Ali's budget of 1947, which was designed to hit hard the Hindu commercial classes, who were strong supporters of the Congress. The government would have broken up but for the British announcement on 20 February 1947 to leave India by June 1948 and the appointment of Lord Mountbatten as the new viceroy. It was also considered imperative to have a national government functioning until the final transfer power to Indians.

The British decision to quit India by June 1948 had a disastrous effect on the situation in Punjab. The Muslim League launched a campaign of direct action which led to the collapse of Khizar Tiwana's coalition government. The communal riots in my hometown, Lahore, and other towns left a legacy of hatred and mistrust among the communities. After hectic and exhaustive negotiations from March to May 1947 with the Indian political leaders, Mountbatten announced the Partition Plan on 3 June 1947. It envisaged the Partition of India into two independent states – India and Pakistan – and also the Partition of the two provinces of Punjab and Bengal. Further, the date of transfer of power was advanced to 15 August 1947. The advancing of the date was an ill-judged decision which contributed considerably to the devastating massacres and destruction of property on both sides of Punjab. The exodus of Hindus and Sikhs, which had begun in April, was now full-scale. Many of them from Lahore locked up their homes and believed they would return when things settled down with the restoration of peace and harmony. That was not to be. The British divided and quit India on 15 August. The Boundary Commission chaired by Sir Cyril Radcliffe was entrusted with the task of demarcating the boundary lines between the two Punjabs. It submitted its award to the viceroy on 12 August but it was made public only on 18 August so as not to disturb the Independence Day celebrations in India and Pakistan.

I was a witness to the chain of events. The spectre of Partition was there but most of us did not think of leaving Lahore even if it became part of Pakistan. Besides, the economy of Lahore was dominated by the Hindus and Sikhs, who owned over 75 per cent of the city's property. This induced the hope that Lahore might be included in India. The boundary award created the Wagah border with Lahore as a part of Pakistan. The large-scale killings on both sides led to the massive evacuation of non-Muslims from Lahore, entire West Punjab, and the Muslims from East Punjab.

My brothers and sisters had joined me in Delhi in July but my parents stayed on in Lahore. My father, a government employee, chose Pakistan since he had no intention of leaving Lahore. But the communal rioting became so widespread that by the beginning of August nearly three-fourths of the Hindu and Sikh population had left Lahore. There was no safe locality and many people moved to a special camp set up at the DAV College, Lahore. It is ironical that Mahatma Gandhi visited Lahore on 6 August, when the bulk of the Hindu population had already left the city, and declared that the rest of his life would be spent in Pakistan which might be East Bengal, West Punjab or the North-West Frontier Province (NWFP). He added: 'I am grieved to learn that people are running away from West Punjab and I am told that Lahore is being evacuated by non-Muslims … If you think Lahore is dead or is dying, do not run away from it but die with what you think is dying Lahore.' I remember how this statement was condemned and ridiculed by practically all of us whose kith and kin were struggling to escape from the city. It was on 14 August that some Muslim friends escorted my parents to the railway station and somehow managed to put them in a compartment occupied by some Englishmen who were kind enough to provide them with a hiding place under their berths. The stabbing incidents were in full swing on the railway platforms. This was the last train to steam out of Lahore as the train services were suspended thereafter. It took nearly ten hours to reach Amritsar. All communications were mostly cut off. Many of us in Delhi anxiously awaited some news of our dear ones stranded in Pakistan. It took more than two weeks to find out that my parents were safe in Amritsar and that my father was on his way to join his postal department office at Ambala Cantonment.

Soon after the announcement of the Partition Plan on 3 June, Government of India employees were given an option to serve either of the two dominions of India and Pakistan. Practically the entire Muslim staff of all ranks – from a peon to the gazetted officer – opted for Pakistan. Nearly 2,000 of them went over to Karachi, the new capital of Pakistan, and by the first week of August 1947, the Pakistan government began functioning in Karachi. I remember the farewell party for the departing colleagues in the commerce department. On a personal note, it was a sad moment when my old classmates and friends Amanullah Sardar and Aslam Hayat left for Karachi. We had parted with assurances to meet again at Lahore, our common hometown; a wish never fulfilled. Sardar retired as principal information officer and Hayat as economic advisor of the Pakistani government. Both are no more.

The Indian officers of the armed forces led by Major General Cariappa gave a farewell party on 6 August to the Pakistani officers headed by Brigadier Raza. It was attended by Viceroy Mountbatten, Pandit Nehru and Defence Minister Sardar Baldev Singh. It is interesting to recall General Cariappa's address on this occasion when he said, 'We now serve in two different armed forces but we fervently hope that nothing anyone says or does will mar the continuation of our present spirit of friendship and comradeship. We hope that God will give us the ability, the strength and the wisdom to serve our respective governments and in such a manner that together we shall provide the essential security for the people of this vast subcontinent.' Unfortunately, the post-Independence history of nearly seven decades is replete with armed conflicts between the two countries.

Colourful celebrations were held all over the country on 15 August 1947, heralding the emergence of India as an independent nation. The new cabinet of the Union of India was sworn in which consisted of the following:

Pandit Jawaharlal Nehru: Prime minister; External and Commonwealth Relations, Scientific Research.

Sardar Vallabhbhai Patel: Home, Information and Broadcasting, States.

Dr Rajendra Prasad: Food and Agriculture.

Maulana Abul Kalam Azad: Education.

Dr John Mathai: Railways and Transport.

Sardar Baldev Singh: Defence.

Mr Jagjivan Ram: Labour.

Mr C.H. Bhabha: Commerce.

Mr Rafi Ahmed Kidwai: Communications.

Rajkumari Amrit Kaur: Health.

Dr B.R. Ambedkar: Law.

R.K. Shanmukham Chetty: Finance.

Dr Syama Prasad Mookerjee: Industries and Supplies.

Mr N.V. Gadgil: Works, Mines and Power.

Even after 15 August, communal rioting and killings continued in both East and West Punjab. Organized evacuation with military escorts from both sides was now taken up by the two governments. The great migration began involving an exchange of more than a million people on each side. It was an operation unprecedented in size, calling forth all the organizational ability of the military and civil authorities.

By the beginning of September 1947, Delhi was flooded with refugees from Punjab. There was an acute shortage of housing in

Delhi. The exodus of about 2,000 officers and clerks was more than balanced by an influx of over 3,000 from Pakistan comprising the staff of the railways, Posts and Telegraph Department and other Central government offices who had decided to opt for India.

I was then living as a sub-tenant of a Punjabi family in the Western Extension Area, a new residential complex off Pusa Road which had come up during World War II. Quite a few houses in the area had been requisitioned by the government and allotted to its officials. Ours was a three-bedroom house with a total of six occupants but after July 1947, with the addition of refugee family members, we were now over twenty clustered in the same house.

By the first week of September, with the influx of over a lakh refugees in Delhi, the communal situation became tense. There was rioting in some parts of the old city. Soon communal conflict flared up and there was widespread arson, looting and killing, besides bomb explosions, in many parts of Delhi. In addition to the police, troops were called out and the situation was brought under control. I vividly remember how the bulk of Muslim families were driven out from their homes on Ajmal Khan Road and some other areas of Karol Bagh.

Here I would like to cite the case of a Muslim family, our immediate neighbours whom we managed to protect. A family of three, Mr Khan, an executive engineer, with his wife and grown-up daughter were occupying the government-requisitioned house. Some antisocial elements and the groups of refugees were actively involved in attacking Muslim houses identified by the local goons. It was on the night of 7 September that we came to know their house would be attacked in the morning. We gave them shelter for the night and early in the morning our neighbour, a Sikh gentleman, drove Mr Khan's car and took his family safely to Imperial Hotel on Queensway. An hour later, the house was ransacked by the goons, who rebuked us for aiding in their escape. The well-to-do Muslim families in New Delhi sought refuge in this hotel before moving to Pakistan. Not only government servants but a vast majority of educated Muslims of different callings from both Old and New Delhi had decided to go to Pakistan for brighter prospects.

The East Punjab government established itself at Simla and so also the high court. Hence government officials and the lawyers' community went to Simla. Most of the other refugees from Lahore landed in Delhi. Not accustomed to living in small towns they preferred Delhi to other cities in East Punjab. The leading shop owners of Anarkali and Mall Road in Lahore also came to set up their businesses in Delhi. Most of them were keen to find a place but only a handful of shops in Connaught Place and other areas were evacuated by the Muslims. The solitary case of timely exchange of business premises in Connaught Place was that of Janki Dass & Co. Among others I recall Raja Bros, cloth merchants, and Rama Krishna & Co., booksellers, who were allotted evacuee shops in Connaught Place. The biggest chemist shop of Punjab, Beli Ram & Co., got a small shop in Gole Market. A few others got allotments in Chandni Chowk. Some enterprising businessmen without shops occupied the verandahs of CP to carry on their trade. The most prominent were the cloth merchants outside Grindlays Bank. The verandah shops dealt in practically everything from dried fruit to stationery. Above all, they offered competitive prices which affected the business of old, established shopkeepers. The latter made complaints and sought their removal from the verandahs in front of their shops but the municipal authorities declined to take any action.

The biggest problem for refugees was housing. Even the well-known wealthy families failed to get allotment of the handful of evacuee properties in New Delhi. The palatial bungalow of

Muhammad Ali Jinnah at 10 Aurangzeb Road had been bought by Seth R.K. Dalmia and the one owned by Liaqat Ali Khan at Hardinge Avenue (Tilak Marg) was taken over by the Pakistan high commission. My close friend Sunder Singh, owner of 'Dingha Singh Building', which is still the landmark of Mall Road, Lahore, was allotted a portion of a small bungalow at Hailey Road. Even rented accommodation was difficult to find. Many refugees from Lahore, with ample resources or regular employment, moved to the newly developed Western Extension Area off Pusa Road and Karol Bagh residential zones.

In order to help refugees in resettlement, a new Ministry of Relief and Rehabilitation was established. The Refugee Information Bureau was also set up in P Block at Raisina Road. I recall how this office attracted crowds of refugees and presented a 'mela' all day.

A welcome fallout of the refugee resettlement was the opening of Camp College in M.B. High School premises at Gole Market. Manned by professors and lecturers from Lahore colleges, it held classes in the evening for courses upto MA degree. It not only fulfilled the needs of refugee students but also offered an opportunity to working persons to upgrade their educational qualifications in hope for a better tomorrow.

8

Japan: Expense Account Paradise

I LANDED IN TOKYO ON 20 June 1956 after my maiden sea voyage on S.S. *Santhia* of the British India Steamship Company. Sailing from Calcutta on 19 May, the sea journey to Japan took four weeks with stopovers at Rangoon, Penang, Singapore, Hong Kong and finally Kobe from where an overnight train took me to Tokyo. It was an enjoyable travel-cum-holiday experience before joining duties in our embassy, then housed in a commercial building at the city centre not far from the famous Ginza, a shopping and entertainment hub. Japan was then going through massive post-war reconstruction at a rapid pace. It was said that General Douglas MacArthur, the supreme commander of Allied forces, hailed as the last shogun, played a dominant role in the making of modern Japan and restoring its position in world trade and economy.

By 1956, Japan had rebuilt its infrastructure and heavy industry to a great extent and was emerging as a major player in world trade. India's trade with Japan had grown over the years with India emerging as one of the major importers of Japanese steel products and machine tools.

Ambassador B.R. Sen, ICS, held regular morning meetings with his diplomatic officers comprising First Secretary (Political) A.K. Dhar, Military Attaché Col. A.C. Chatterjee, Press Attaché P. Dass, First Secretary (Commercial) D. Hejmadi, Third Secretary (Commercial) A.S. Chib and and myself, the second secretary (commercial). I found these meetings to be most educative. Ambassador Sen was a zealous proponent of expanding and strengthening our economic and political ties with Japan. Once, I recall his informing us that he had not succeeded in persuading Prime Minister Nehru to not treat Japan as an American colony and ignore its importance while strengthening our ties with China. Those were the days of 'Hindi-Chini bhai-bhai'.

As regards bilateral trade exchanges, our major export to Japan was iron ore. In fact, Japan was the leading buyer and had established a steel makers' union to deal with the large number of Indian exporters. The Japanese monopoly position as a buyer greatly enhanced their bargaining position and Indian suppliers found themselves outmaneuvered. It was around this time that the commerce ministry decided to nationalize the export of iron ore through the newly established State Trading Corporation. This improved the Indian bargaining position and the two monopoly bodies came to conclude long-term bulk contracts at fair prices. The very idea of state trading was inspired by the Japanese. On the imports side, Indian Railways were one of the major buyers of Japanese steel rails and wheel sets. Three Indian railway engineers were posted in Japan at different locations to undertake pre-shipment inspection of the goods as per contract terms.

Before World War II, a good number of Indian traders had established themselves at Kobe and Yokohama. Most of them handled the export of Japanese textiles to South-East Asian trade hubs of Hong Kong and Singapore as well as India. The Japanese were dependent on them since Indians had their extensive network and direct contacts with the wholesale traders in all principal cities. Besides, the Japanese were handicapped owing to their lack of knowledge of the English language and also of the prevalent trading practices and customer preferences. In post-war years, when the Japanese expanded their production with new, modern textile factories, they conceived a novel plan to enhance their export earnings by cutting down the middlemen profits. They inserted a leaflet inside every carton or package informing the final buyer that he would get the same goods at a discounted price if he placed orders directly with the specified Japanese company. This in turn adversely affected the lucrative textile trade carried on by local Indians. By the mid-1950s their numbers had dropped and very few were left at Kobe and Yokohama. Some enterprising Indians, however, tied up with Japanese companies exporting new products such as photo equipment, electronics, machine tools and other engineering goods.

The post-war emergence of Japan as a major economic power bears testimony to the nation's determination, hard work, integrity, spirit of sacrifice and, above all, its people's ardent and heroic patriotism. The American role in it was also an important factor with nearly a hundred thousand US troops stationed in Japan. Unlike the other Allied powers – British and French – Americans were allowed by General MacArthur to fraternize with the Japanese. The tourism industry also flourished with Japan emerging as a favourite destination for Americans. Japan also became a holiday destination for thousands of American army personnel then stationed in Korea. Significant steps were taken to strengthen the Japanese currency. American money was worthless until it had been exchanged for army scrip or yen at 360 yen to the dollar – a rate which had been set by General MacArthur.

The Japanese automobile industry was still in its infant stages, having a low priority in the overall export-oriented industrial development. At that time two European small cars – Hillman and Renault – had assembly plants. The business elite used American cars. Japanese roads were in a poor state as the railways were given the highest priority for transport.

The cost of living in Japan during the mid-1950s was practically the same as in India. I had a three-bedroom, double-storey house with a garage, a small garden and maids quarters located in a neighbourhood popular with diplomats, and its monthly rent was Rs 800 only. My foreign allowance as a second secretary had a provision for engaging two full-time local maids. A number of Japanese consumer products were meant only for export and denied to the home market. Supplies to the diplomatic corps were termed as 'domestic export'. The Commonwealth diplomats also had access to the British embassy canteen, a duty-free source for imported groceries and dairy products not available in the local market. It was indeed a world of luxury and in my entire career abroad I never enjoyed such luxury and comfort again.

The Japanese business companies' mode of functioning was unique and so was their work culture. In our business negotiations, I found the Japanese tough but extremely polite. They believed in prolonging every discussion in order to exhaust the patience of the opposite side and strike the best bargain. I found it educative. The post-war Japanese industry aimed at high-quality production in order to compete with Europe and the USA. It took dynamic steps to stamp out the pre-war tag of cheap and poor quality for Japanese goods. The show windows of stores presented an interesting display of all kinds of imported goods including menswear along with the comparable Japanese products with competitive prices. In the field of consumer electronics, they were emerging as leaders in the manufacture and export of transistor radios, tape recorders and sound equipment. In the field of cameras, photo equipment and material, the Japanese brands of Canon, Nikon, Konica, Yashica and Fuji had attained global reputation. Their renovated and new department stores like Mitsukoshi, Takashimaya and Daimaru mirrored the amazing Japanese progress in consumer goods both in variety and quality.

In day-to-day life, I was struck by the honesty of ordinary Japanese and their total refusal to accept any tips. I recall how once a taxi driver drove all the way to my house to return a silver tumbler and milk bottle we had left in the cab and he declined to accept any reward. I had a delightful experience when I went for a test to obtain a Japanese driving licence. Even after a few attempts, I was not able to reverse my car on the prescribed circular track. I told the inspector in my broken Japanese that I always asked my wife to go out of the car and guide my reversing. He laughed and remarked that he was not familiar with this Indian practice and gave me the driving licence. I have preserved it since then and also used it to get local driving licences in other countries.

I discovered some striking features of Japanese society. They had developed an acute sense of propriety of form which played an intimidating role in their day-to-day life. A keen observance of the correct 'form' was a symbol of accomplishment. It was a little surprising to find that in their workplace, 'equal pay for equal work' was neither practised nor sought. It was not competence but only seniority that counted in promotion. Besides, the Japanese trade unions worked hand in glove with the management to generate higher productivity and lower costs. That is how workers' strike was a rare phenomenon. Their principle goal of life was to achieve harmony by understanding the precept of interdependence in society with mutual obligations and responsibilities.

After the war, there was a notable increase in women in the workforce. Young Japanese girls were employed as conductors, salesgirls, waitresses, office clerks and interpreters. Japanese companies also employed young attractive girls who served *ocha* (tea) to senior executives at frequent intervals. I learnt that this task was reserved only for the young and on crossing early twenties they were transferred to other duties in the office. In leading stores I also came across efficient, pleasant and polite salesgirls including some carrying a tag 'I speak English'.

Japanese women as a rule were excluded from business parties, and gracefully accepted this custom. In fact, they expected their husbands to be part of such male gatherings. Returning home late meant that the husband was successful and going up the ladder in his career. It was believed that Japanese women, accustomed to pampering the male ego, made excellent wives. No wonder, many American soldiers and civilians got attracted to them and looked for Japanese brides. The clever Japanese showed their ingenuity by setting up shops of letter writers to enable Japanese girls lacking the knowledge of English to correspond with their American boyfriends. They introduced crash courses for learning English (they called it American) and even opened 'American Bride Schools' to train the girls in the American way of life. They were taught the use of knife and fork and to develop taste for American staple dishes. Further, they were instructed in donning American formal and informal attire. The course also included imparting knowledge of American etiquette, customs and manners. After completing the course they had to pass a test. I remember witnessing an assemblage of girls in gowns undergoing the test in the reserved dining hall of Imperial Hotel, Kobe. During the 1950s thousands of Americans returned home with Japanese brides.

Alarmed by the high birth rate in the post-war years, the Japanese government recognized family planning as an integral part of the overall population policy. The planned parent movement was vigorously supported by official and public institutions as a means to solve Japan's serious population problem. It was then generally recognized that Japan was an overpopulated country and it was imperative to introduce birth control and promote emigration. It was around this time that some major Japanese companies financed the migration of Japanese workers to Brazil, which needed manpower to develop its agricultural sector. Incidentally, India then had declined the Brazilian offer. Personally interested in the subject of family planning, I contacted the Family Planning Federation of Japan and became a friend of their vice-president, Dr Kan Majima, a knowledgeable and interesting gentleman. He was conversant with the Indian government's measures for family planning. He was instrumental in legalizing induced abortion in Japan and had trained over a thousand Japanese doctors in his novel operation technique. He told me that the cost of the operation came to only around 3,000 Yen or less than ten dollars, and the woman could return home by bus or train, two to three hours after the operation. He had a great sense of humour and told me that he was promoting American tourism to Japan since the cost of abortion including the air travel expense worked out at far less than what they would spend on an illegal abortion in the USA. Dr Majima had also specialized in the reversible vasectomy operation. Quite a few Americans came to him for this operation and he charged only ten dollars. He told me laughing that when they asked him to give a certificate for showing it to their sex-mates for more enjoyable sex, he demanded an additional twenty dollars.

A memorable experience worth mentioning was the short audience with Emperor Hirohito on the New Year's Day of 1957. As per tradition, the entire diplomatic corps was invited to the emperor's palace for the new year celebration over a cup of sake. The diplomats, led by ambassadors, would walk in a single file, stop for a second in front of the emperor, exchange greetings and move on. I vividly remember that I made a faux pas and shook hands with the emperor which was the privilege of ambassadors only. It was a majestic and glamorous event with some diplomats in their colourful national costumes and the Japanese elite in their formal tailcoats. The royal ambience added to the flavour of the warm sake in tiny cups with a bluish figure of a flying duck in the centre. Emperor Hirohito was always hailed as a mystic figure in the royal species until 1 January 1946, when by a proclamation he renounced his claim to divinity. Under the pre-War constitution, the emperor was described as the symbol of the state and of the unity of the people. Adored as 'sacred and inviolate', the emperor was the fountainhead of all sovereignty whence power could be drawn by service chiefs and the cabinet. Therefore, the august presence of the emperor lent a special aura to the occasion which turned even more alluring when guests were told to carry the sake cups with them as an imperial gift.

Having heard a lot about the extraordinary Japanese social and cultural scene, I turned a keen observer of their artistic way of life. I was struck by their passion for creating beauty everywhere: in their homes, gardens, shrines and monuments. For me, it was a strange new world, in a strange new setting. I was deeply impressed by the grace, politeness and decorum of the Japanese people, irrespective of their station in life. They represented a wonderful amalgam of tradition and modernity. Apparently westernized in their tailcoats in public, they would be seen at home in their kimonos squatting on the tatami (matted) floor. The same was visible on the entertainment scene with the age-old Kabuki theatre in Tokyo enjoying the same patronage and popularity as the neighbouring Nichigeki music hall with semi-nude Japanese dancing beauties entertaining the visitors. Coming to drinks, their traditional sake coexisted with beer, wine and whiskey. The famous beer brands had their outlets in Ginza, the centre of Tokyo, where fresh, foaming beer from the brewery's pipeline was served. The Japanese boasted about their much publicized whiskey brand 'Gold Nikka' though it was no match to Scotch whisky. The popular drink for an average Japanese was beer. The elite interacting with foreigners enjoyed taking Scotch but their capacity was rather limited when compared with other Asians.

At night, Tokyo put on a new face. The Ginza and other amusement districts with their cafes, bars, tea houses, nightclubs and music halls would open their doors to pleasure-seekers. Some of them advertised their offerings: 'Consoling company to lonely hearts and thirsty souls'. On stepping in, one was greeted by a row of glamorous hostesses ready to be selected for company. It was not unusual to see a colourful old Japanese engaging two of them to take care of him. There were some exclusive nightclubs where no foreigner was admitted. In bars as well, one would find young girls around, ready to be invited for drinks and company.

The Japanese are extraordinary people. Famous for their dedication to hard work, they also took relaxation seriously. They had therefore built varied entertainment for men, and their thriving sex industry did not lag behind in their crusade for innovation. There were brothel inmates, Turkish bath girls, hostesses in bars, tea houses, and nightclubs. For love nests, hotels provided rooms on an hourly basis with the tariff conspicuously displayed outside. Around 1970, I read about an ingenious Japanese entrepreneur who had even set up a mistress bank and enrolled members, both men and women. He arranged suitable partners for company and sexual coupling on mutually negotiated terms and conditions. The most astounding novelty, once illustratively reported in an English tabloid, was the Japanese craze for eating tasty delicacies served on the body frame of a young girl wearing nothing but a smile. A simple dish of sushi on a human plate would cost $300, ten times the normal rate.

At the top of the entertainment scene was, of course, the geisha, who lent grace and charm to the exquisite soirees of the wealthy and influential elite. Thanks to the patronage of the rich and powerful elite, the 'flower and willow world' of the geisha had endured through the ages. So well known is the word 'geisha' in the world, yet so little understood. The chief attraction of the geisha lies in the word 'gei' (accomplishment). Combined with 'sha' it stands for an accomplished professional entertainer. She is usually highly cultured, exquisitely dressed, and delicately mannered, and has a knowledge not only of the past and bygone elegance but of contemporary gossip. Her main function is to provide an atmosphere of chic and gaiety. It is not on her skill in the art of love, but on her skills in singing, dancing and conversation that her reputation rests.

Amusement with a geisha was a popular pastime, but in the post-war years her functions were taken over by the nightclub and bar hostesses who catered to the needs of the ordinary people. As times changed, the geisha came to be associated with tradition, as a symbol of its aesthetic culture, and only those appreciative of an old lifestyle and willing to pay the high expense involved continued to draw upon the services of the geisha for adding special grace and charm to their parties.

Japan has been acclaimed as the world's greatest expense account paradise. Most of the geisha parties were organized by business tycoons for politicians, officials and important foreign guests. The Japanese companies trading with India would invite us to the special tea houses and restaurants with charming kimono-clad hostesses and attendants. These were exclusive spots patronized by their company. My senior colleague, a teetotaller, usually avoided attending such male parties. The hosts found in me a willing guest since I knew very well that I was just as much a gift of God to them as they were a gift of God to me. I was an excuse for them to enjoy an evening on expense account. Besides, I returned their hospitality by inviting them to my parties at home. This way I was able to visit quite a few exclusive places where kimono-clad hostesses were invariably in attendance.

I vividly remember my maiden experience of traditional geisha entertainment with my Japanese hosts. As we entered the premises, we were helped by a beautiful kimonoed attendant to take off our shoes. We were then profusely greeted with words of welcome by the mama-san, the wise mentor of the geishas. We were surrounded by lovely attendants who seated us upon kneeling cushions. Each guest became the charge of one of them as she sat noiselessly by his side to serve him. The lacquered services were laid on the low table. They were smiling and flirting, as if in a dream, while pouring warm sake into the cup of each guest with delightful grace and dexterity. Then all, at once, with a little burst of laughter two young beauties entered, made the customary prostration of greeting and sat in front of us. They were pretty and dressed in costly kimonos made of brocade and silk with golden obis. They were girdled like queens with faces painted white like porcelain. The artistically arranged towering hair of each was decked with fresh flowers, wonderful combs and pins and with curious ornaments of gold. They greeted us as if they had always known us; they jested, laughed and uttered funny little cries. These were geishas, who with their smiles and play of eyes soon created a hallowed atmosphere making everything appear wondrous and blissful. To me they appeared like apsaras from heaven as they dazzled me with their beauty, grace and charm. They joined us in a general chat for a few minutes on such topics as sport, kabuki, business and even politics, which I could not follow much as my knowledge of Japanese was rather limited. Soon, they glided into the open space at the farther end of the room and began singing and dancing. Their dance consisted wholly of graceful posturing. Two of them were dancing together with such synchronized steps and gestures as only years of training could render possible. It was more like acting accompanied by a delightful waving of sleeves and fans and with a play of eyes and features – sweet, subtle and subdued. I gathered that they were relating some legend with the accompaniment of the samisen and a tiny drum played by a small girl sitting in a corner.

The maidens in attendance on us continued pouring sake – that warm, pale rice wine which filled the veins with soft contentment – creating a faint sense of ecstasy through which the world seemed to become a happier place and the geishas seemed like maids of Paradise as their voices rippled out with alluring sweetness the words of an ancient song. Our happiness grew, but as midnight drew near, the tinkling sound of the samisen faded away and the geishas joined us to resume conversation. I was amazed at their repartee and wit. As we were about to part, I requested my hosts to convey my deep appreciation of their enchanting performance and how I was stirred by their stunning beauty and charm. As we got up to leave, both of them escorted us to the door with parting bows and laughing cries of 'sayonara'.

After a study of the geisha institution, I learnt that the concept demonstrates the Japanese ingenuity for gratifying human desire with an illusion of love mixed with youth and grace, but without regrets and responsibilities. A geisha appears at a party only as a 'human flower'; to be looked at, not to be touched. She can enchant you with her music and dance, conversation and wit, but no sexual advance is permissible. The familiarity which foreign guests at times permit themselves with geishas, though endured with smiling patience, was considered by the Japanese as a sign of vulgarity. Companionship with a geisha can lead to a sexual union after one is accepted as a patron or danna who then develops a private and exclusive relationship. The patron has to provide for the maintenance expenses of his playmate and confidante. The actual financial arrangement is handled most discreetly and never revealed to anyone. As a rule, the patron pays all the geisha's bills and when the original arrangement is concluded he also pays a substantial commission to the mama-san.

This brings to mind the somewhat similar institution of 'ganika' in ancient India. The ganika had to be accomplished in sixty-four kalas (arts) which included dancing and singing. She enjoyed a respectable status in royal courts and was invited to the gatherings of scholars and poets. She entertained the rich and famous who vied with one another to win her favour. Though marriage was ruled out, the ganika too, like the geisha, had her patron wealthy enough to maintain her under a mutual agreement. In both cases, there was harmonious coexistence with the patron's wife as there was a clear division of their respective social roles. With so much in common, perhaps along with Buddhism, the ganika institution also spread to the Far East with the word ganika transformed into geisha.

9

First Stint with the STC

I HAD TO CUT SHORT MY term in Tokyo and seek premature transfer due to a family tragedy. On my return to Delhi in October 1957, K.B. Lal, then joint secretary and chairman of the State Trading Corporation (STC), was kind enough to send me on deputation to the Corporation. Established in May 1956 to promote India's foreign trade, its first major activity was to handle export of minerals, especially iron ore, which was canalized through it. When I went to report to the managing director, D. Sandilya, a fine gentleman, I was pleasantly surprised to learn that they had already decided to post me as deputy divisional manager in-charge of iron ore procurement from all over India. I was greatly impressed by the briefing I received from Mr Sandilya and have fond memories of working with him. My experience in Japan and acquaintance with the Japanese companies importing iron ore worked in my favour.

Within a short period of one year the STC had set up an extensive network with branch offices in Calcutta, Bombay and Madras to supervise iron ore shipments from these ports. I was given the responsibility of concluding purchase contracts with iron ore suppliers. There were established exporters who supplied iron ore either free on board (f.o.b.) or free on rail (f.o.r.) basis. There were small mine owners and traders who offered iron ore stocks at the railway sidings and still others at the mine head. I was entrusted with the task of framing a comprehensive policy to ensure timely deliveries from different categories of suppliers. It was a teething period for the public sector which was now spreading its wings in different fields of the Indian economy. There was much excitement all around as we felt we were working for a momentous national enterprise.

The STC's office was then located in a rented bungalow in Golf Links area and I was allotted a room on the second floor which was in fact a barsati converted into an office. My immediate boss was Mr B.K. Kochar, general manager of the mineral division, who knew me well, having met me in Tokyo during his official visit. It was a joy working with him as we sat late hours every day. There was total dedication to work and a realization that we were performing a very important task to enable the success of the emerging public sector.

In order to formulate a comprehensive iron ore procurement policy, I travelled all over the country visiting mining areas in the east, west and south, and exploring the transport network by rail and road to the ports. I recommended that the STC should establish direct contacts with the mine owners and deal only with those trading companies who held mining leases in their own name. I encouraged small mine owners in south India from Veldurti to Bellary–Hospet to form cooperative societies and secure long-term bulk contracts from the STC. There were small ports like Cuddalore, Mangalore, Karwar and Belikeri, where midstream loading was done on ships. I recall how we developed the road transport from Hubli to Karwar port. Besides, I got so involved with my work that I learnt to guess the approximate ferrous content of iron ore by observing and handling the piece in my hand.

The introduction of iron ore procurement policy as framed by me annoyed some trading companies who used to exploit small mine owners. On the other hand, quite a few cooperatives of small mine owners encouraged and supported by the STC were happy. They were facilitated to supply on f.o.r. basis. In this way, the role of middlemen who had political contacts in Delhi was adversely affected. I recall the case of an eminent business person known to the commerce secretary N. Ranganathan whose company was denied a contract. They had been in the iron ore business for several years but without any mining lease in their name. When Sandilya was told to look into the matter he sent me to the commerce secretary to explain our policy. It is heartening to record that the secretary heard my explanation and supported the STC's decision. In another case, the commerce minister, Morarji Desai, ordered us to give an iron ore contract to some party. But when informed that they were not qualified to receive a contract unless the policy approved by the government was altered, the minister did not pursue the matter further. My purpose in recounting these small incidents is to highlight the state of affairs in the public sector at that time. The STC then had little interference from the political elite or the ministry's officialdom. It enjoyed autonomy to carry on its activities within the framework of approved policy guidelines.

By the middle of 1958 the iron ore procurement network was well established. I recall my memorable tour in the mining areas of south India when I travelled by road from Madras to Bangalore and then all the way to Mangalore port, covering Karwar and also the wayside, newly developed, small Belikeri port. I was overwhelmed by the reception at every point by small mine owners of cooperative societies which I had been instrumental in setting up. It was the first and last time I ever travelled so extensively in that part of the country. Later, I also visited the major mining areas in Orissa and Bengal.

Apart from Japan, we exported iron ore to Poland and Czechoslovakia which had large steel plants set up with Soviet collaboration. They were dependent on low-grade Russian iron ore but imported high-grade ore from India. The mechanism of 'Rupee Trade' agreements with them had promoted our exports. The late 1950s witnessed an expansion of India's trade and economic relations with Soviet bloc countries. The Soviet Union emerged as a promising market not only for our traditional exports like tea, coffee, jute, hides and skins, and textiles but also consumer products. India was then facing shortage of foreign exchange and at the same time wanted to establish a strong industrial base with steel plants, machine tools, power equipment and other engineering industries. The Soviet Union was the first country to assist us in our development plans through credits and bilateral Rupee Payment Agreements. As foreign trade was a state monopoly in the Soviet Union and other East European countries, we had to deal with state enterprises in those countries. The business and trade division of STC soon established contacts with corresponding state enterprises of those countries.

To achieve industrial development and sustained economic growth, it was imperative for India to broaden the structure of exports by increasing the share of non-traditional manufactured products. It was equally important to develop new markets in the socialist countries of East Europe. Bilateral trade and payment agreements with these countries played a vital role in the expansion and diversification of trade exchanges with them. The STC on its part enlarged its operations and began playing a constructive role in promoting exports of both traditional and non-traditional products.

The STC's office shifted from Golf Links in early 1958 and now occupied the entire Saraswati Bhavan building in the middle circle of Connaught Place. Earlier, the STC was chiefly manned by government officials on deputation, but now a number of persons were recruited from the private sector in order to make the Corporation's activities more business-oriented. For more than a year, I was working over ten hours a day with little reward except plenty of appreciation from the managing director, Mr Sandilya. In fact, he strongly recommended my promotion as joint divisional manager based on merit but without success. In the meantime, there was some talk of Mr Sandilya leaving the organization which sapped my enthusiasm for work. Around the same time, I received a communication from the Ministry of External Affairs asking me if I would like to re-opt for absorption in the foreign service. I went to Mr Sandilya to seek his advice and he told me to accept the offer and join the Foreign Office. Accordingly, within a week or so the STC was asked to relieve me for joining duties in the Foreign Office. Mr Sandilya however persuaded them to delay it for a few months so as to enable me to wind up all pending cases and train my successor.

At my farewell party, attended by the entire STC staff, Mr Sandilya profusely lauded my work and valuable contribution in the STC's trading activities. He made a prophetic statement that I would always stand by the STC and take care of its interest on my postings abroad. How true it was, as I did precisely that during my postings abroad in Poland and Yugoslavia, which finally landed me in the lap of the STC again as their chief for East Europe in Moscow ten years later in 1969.

10

Introduction to the Foreign Office

I JOINED THE MINISTRY IN MARCH 1959 as attaché (NEFA). The administration of NEFA (North East Frontier Agency) and NHTA (Naga Hills and Tuensang Area) was under the control of the Ministry of External Affairs. So was the Indian Frontier Administrative Service whose officers were posted there as political officers to run the local administration under the stewardship of the adviser to the governor of Assam, then Mr A.F. Rustomji, ICS. The security of the region was taken care of by the Assam Rifles troops under the command of the inspector general of Assam Rifles, Major General A.S. Guraya. It was around this time that the Dalai Lama with his entourage crossed over to India and was given sanctuary and protection by our officers in NEFA.

A major task undertaken during my time was the reorganization of the Indian Frontier Administrative Service. Rules and regulations governing the service were framed to streamline the process of recruitment, training, posting and promotion. A selection board under the chairmanship of the foreign secretary was constituted and in 1960 a batch of thirty officers was selected from amongst the army and civilian candidates.

In late 1960, I was given the charge of undersecretary responsible for the postings and transfers of staff members in our missions abroad and at headquarters. A virtual outsider and not familiar with any staff member, I was unbiased and impartial in the selection of staff members for posting abroad to different stations classified into three categories – A,B and C – depending on the living conditions there. As secretary of the Junior Establishment Board, I would draw up a list of postings strictly in accordance with the prescribed rules and regulations and get it approved by the Board. Those days there was no political interference in these matters, nor did senior officers make any recommendations to favour a particular staff member. After the Board's approval, I would personally go with the list to obtain formal sanction from the deputy minister, Ms Lakshmi Menon, a kind-hearted and generous lady who evinced great interest in the welfare of staff members.

A notable event of my time was the recruitment of lower division clerks through the Employment Exchange. In 1961, we faced an acute shortage of clerical staff in the ministry. The opening of some new missions abroad and increasing staff requirements of some prominent ones had aggravated the staff position. The annual intake through the Union Public Service Commission (UPSC) was limited and the share of the Ministry of External Affairs was small; just enough to take care of retirement vacancies. Another cause of this shortage was the reversion of assistants, clerks and stenographers not absorbed in the ministries' cadre to other government departments. While a few had declined to serve abroad for personal reasons, there were others who were disqualified for having three or more children. The rule on family size restriction was strictly adhered to, resulting in the ministry losing some highly competent and experienced staff members.

To resolve this situation, I recommended an emergency ad hoc recruitment of LDCs through the Delhi Employment Exchange. The selected candidates were to be appointed on a purely temporary basis subject to their replacement by the UPSC recruits. My proposal was approved and the Delhi Employment Exchange was asked to forward the details of the applicants. After preliminary selection, candidates were called for an interview and finally sixty were recruited. Interestingly, over the years they were all permanently absorbed in the IFS(B) and some of them even retired as undersecretaries.

There were some interesting episodes regarding postings of clerks to the UK. There were instances when staff members transferred back to Delhi disappeared with their families and would not show up to catch the boats which had firm bookings. I recall that the Indian government's request to British authorities to trace and deport such persons was ignored by them. Until the 1960s, Commonwealth citizens did not require any visa to enter the UK and they were free to take up local employment. The temptation for a clerk or assistant to settle down in London with a job or some small business was so great that he was willing to forego all his service benefits, pension, gratuity, etc. It was only after the introduction of new immigration restrictions in the 1970s that the situation changed.

This reminds me of an extraordinary case of a clerk who was posted in 1961 to Turkey. He took his entitled advance payments and stated that his family would join him later. He had official passports for himself and his family. After a two-week leave he was supposed to catch a boat from Bombay, but never showed up. Considering that the government's concern was to recover the amount paid to him, I recommended it would be futile to pursue the case as I was informed unofficially that he had landed in London. Thereupon, I summoned his wife who dutifully paid the entire amount received by her husband and I closed the case. I am aware of some cases where the staff members left their families in the USA and returned alone only to take premature retirement, not permissible abroad under some outdated rules involving unnecessary expenditure on travel home.

The diplomatic officers were usually sent on direct postings from one mission to another but staff members were required to return to headquarters after each posting abroad. I observed that they anxiously looked forward to their next transfer abroad. For them the headquarters was a hardship posting.

Funnily, our missions abroad were miniature secretariats. It is a pity that the founding fathers, eminent civil servants otherwise, replicated the administrative structure at home in the missions abroad. Every diplomatic officer was provided with a stenographer when there was no genuine need for it. Then there were accountants, chancery assistants, consular assistants, cipher assistants in every mission irrespective of the volume of work.

I belonged to the Indian Economic Service before joining the Foreign Office. With my economics background and experience in the Ministry of Commerce, I was keen to pursue a career in economic diplomacy, especially after my posting in Tokyo. Having spent over three years at the headquarters, it was time to be posted abroad. I was sounded a couple of times when vacancies came up in some prized stations but I preferred to stay. Finally, I told the joint secretary (administration), Mr Padmanabhan, that I was keen on a commercial posting anywhere in the world. That was a time when IFS officers were usually reluctant to accept commercial assignments except in major capitals like London, Washington or Paris. The Soviet Union and the socialist countries of East Europe were the least popular destinations. When I learnt about the upcoming vacancy of commercial secretary in our mission at Warsaw, I got it with support from the commerce ministry. This meant a return to my parent ministry, where I had already served for more than a decade. Though all commercial posts abroad had been integrated into the IFS cadre, the selection was formally approved by the commerce secretary who was also a member of the Foreign Service Board.

After receiving posting orders, I had a week's briefing at the ministry which included a day each with the STC and the newly formed Minerals and Metal Trading Corporation (MMTC). Mr S. Vohra, ICS, the joint secretary in charge of the Soviet bloc, familiarized me with the current trade and economic relations with Poland and the pending issues. He advised me to study the bilateral Trade and Payment Agreement with Poland and the mechanism of rupee trade. In the STC and MMTC, my old colleagues were happy on my going to Warsaw where they had active business relations with state enterprises. As per established practice, I also visited the Chambers of Commerce in Calcutta and Bombay and met their members engaged in import and export with Poland.

Technically, I was posted as second secretary (commercial). However, considering my extensive experience, and having already served as second secretary (commercial) at Tokyo, the commerce ministry prevailed upon the external affairs ministry to designate me 'commercial secretary' as a special case. This was the start of my long innings as India's trade representative in Soviet bloc countries for over a decade.

The most amusing part of the preparatory exercise before departure was the security briefing in the Ministry of External Affairs. Some section officer from the security wing read out the activities of spy agencies in the communist countries, apparently from some British literature on the subject. He spoke about the honey traps laid by them and how to be vigilant, and avoid them. Then he screened some old, worn-out documentary to illustrate what he was alluding to. The entire exercise was ridiculous and a waste of time, but surely a means to justify the role of the security section.

On the lighter side, the Ministry of External Affairs prided in having a privately owned cafeteria, the famous 'Hira Lal Canteen'. Hira Lal specialized in serving tea, coffee and snacks in exquisite crockery by liveried waiters to the senior officers who received foreign visitors. He was an institution in himself and every one praised him for running the best canteen, perhaps the only private one left in the North and South Blocks. The canteen had a festive look during lunch hour and was a meeting ground for staff members. Hira Lal was generous in extending credit facilities to everyone since he knew they would repay all their debts once they got advances on a foreign posting. He also acted as a banker and cashed the cheques of officers at odd hours, a free service that I also availed in an emergency. I remember enjoying his freshly fried delicious hot pakoras with tea at 4 p.m. He kept different grades of tea sets to match the rank of officers ordering tea.

An unforgettable person was Ramsabad Rai, the peon who worked with me from day one until my last day in the ministry. Most elegantly dressed in official uniform with a neatly tied turban, he belonged to the old generation of Raj days. He knew the art of gaining the confidence of his master. The workload made me sit for late hours in office, which he welcomed since this enabled him to earn overtime allowance. Having served the ministry for over thirty years, he was a virtual storehouse of information about officers and staff members. He had his favourites among the latter and at the opportune moment recommended their cases for desired postings. I had fixed one hour from 4 p.m. to 5 p.m. for the staff members to walk in and present their grievances. Interestingly, he would brief me in advance about their background and problems. Noticing me in a receptive mood, he would also entertain me with office gossip including rumoured affairs of some female staff with their colleagues. Once I fractured my foot and was working from home for over two weeks. He was dutifully in attendance, bringing all files in the morning and carrying them back to office in the evening. As he missed the hurly-burly of office, he was always praying for my early recovery. He retired soon after my departure and went back to his village. After that I had no news about him but I still fondly remember him. He was probably the last member of the fading tribe of the Raj.

11

Poland: Jewel of the Soviet Bloc

A SEA VOYAGE FROM BOMBAY BY SS *ASIA* to Genoa, and a train journey later, on 27 August 1962 I landed at Warsaw. I was lodged at the Bristol Hotel, an old landmark of the city. I stayed there for a month before moving to a villa in Mokotov, a posh residential area of Warsaw. Unlike cities in the West, Warsaw lacked the chaotic scenes of a metropolitan city. I found Polish people easy-going and friendly, with a singular regard for Indians. Those were the glorious days of Indo-Soviet relations, which in turn had brought other socialist countries also closer to India. Poland, the jewel of the communist bloc, followed Moscow in developing trade and economic relations with India. The Soviet bloc focused on India as it served as a window to Third World countries of Asia and Africa, where they were keen to build commercial relations.

The Polish government allotted accommodation to embassies for offices and residences. In the absence of any suitable accommodation, embassies would rent privately owned houses through the government agency Public Management Committee, or PUMA. We had a palatial mansion for the ambassador's residence in Alej Rouz, a prestigious quarter of Warsaw. The chancery was housed in a double-storey villa allotted to us by the government in Zoliborz. The staff members were all accommodated in state-owned apartment buildings. As no government housing was available for me, our embassy had already booked a villa under construction for a monthly rent of 9,000 zlotys (Rs 1,800). The lease was signed with two documents, one specifying the rent payable to PUMA, i.e., 4,500 zlotys, and the other for the actual rent of 9,000 zlotys agreed to with the landlord for our official record. The difference between the two amounting to 4,500 zlotys per month was paid in cash to the landlord for the entire lease period of three years. This was an accepted practice followed by foreign missions in Warsaw. All documentation was finalized in consultation with a Polish lawyer who acted as a legal adviser.

Soon after my taking over, the Indian trade delegation led by S. Vohra, ICS, arrived to conclude the Annual Trade Protocol under the Trade and Payment Agreement which stipulated annual meetings alternatively in New Delhi and Warsaw. The protocol embodied a comprehensive list of export and import items by both sides with a specified volume or value to work out a balance in mutual trade turnover. The unit of account for settlement was agreed to be the Indian rupee. That is how the term 'Rupee Trade' came into vogue. Though the traders quoted their prices in US dollars, the payments were credited to bank accounts in rupees at the official rate of exchange. In order to promote their export of machinery and equipment, Poland followed Moscow and extended credits to India repayable through Indian exports. The two major items which involved intensive negotiations were steel products in the Polish export list and Indian oilcakes in their import list. A leading meat exporter of East Europe, Poland had a vast demand for oilcakes which served as cattle feed. India, on the other hand, badly needed steel products for its railways and other industrial projects. This was followed by another delegation led by Y. T. Shah, joint secretary, Ministry of Finance, who concluded a credit agreement with Poland to finance their export of machinery and equipment to India.

The Polish planned economy gave priority to heavy industry and did not pay due attention to the consumer goods sector. There was shortage of supplies, and products lacked variety and quality. Imported products were sometimes available at private shops at exorbitant prices. There was a government store that sold imported goods against free foreign exchange which some Polish citizens received through remittances from their friends and relations abroad. Poland was a member of the Council of Mutual Economic Assistance (CMEA) set up in 1949 to promote economic integration among the Soviet bloc countries. An interesting feature of intra-CMEA trade was the 'variety exchange', which envisaged an exchange of similar range of products of equivalent value amongst the members.

The Polish economy was run on multiple exchange rates of their currency 'zloty'. There was an official rate for US dollar for a bank zloty, another one almost three times for cash zloty and still another one was the market rate. For a newcomer it was confusing. The Polish duty-free store Baltona offered a variety of imported as well as Polish products against payment in foreign exchange. The pricing system of Polish goods in foreign exchange was so complex that several exchange rates were applied according to the product category, i.e., whether these were necessaries or luxuries.

The Polish industry and trade were both under state monopoly but a good part of the agriculture was privately owned and farmers were allowed to sell a part of their produce in the open market. There was also a shopping cluster in the centre of the city with a chain of private shops stocked with imported goods which they would buy and sell. Poles were also allowed to legally sell gifted foreign liquor and cigarettes to government shops.

Though Polish people enjoyed greater freedom than those in other socialist counties, their interaction with foreigners was under surveillance. Those in state trading enterprises were allowed to visit foreigners with whom they had official dealings. Only professional artists enjoyed the freedom to socialize with foreigners. I went out of the way to cultivate these sources and broaden my contacts for securing a marriage of culture and commerce. This proved to be rewarding during my long innings in the communist countries. In order to promote trade relations, it was important to build personal contacts with officials of state enterprises. For this, I tried to trace officials and business representatives who had done a posting in India. I found them friendly and helpful.

One of the major trade events in East Europe was the annual international trade fair held in the month of June in the Polish city of Poznan. Apart from trade, it was a great East–West meeting ground, and India was also a regular participant. I used to set up my camp office there to provide assistance to Indian businessmen participating in the fair. During the fair, Poznan city looked festive and attracted large crowds from West Europe. Those days, foreign travel for Indians was highly restricted and participation in the Poznan fair was a valid excuse to get the famous 'P' form. There were a few regulars who came to conclude sale contracts under the fair quota introduced by the Ministry of Foreign Trade to attract participants. There were others who just showed their faces on the opening or the 'India Day' reception and then vanished for holidaying in Europe. The Indian pavilion was a great attraction for enjoying a cup of tea and cashew nuts. Poles were great tea drinkers. They called it *herbata* and preferred to take it without milk. Another attraction were Polish beauties clad in saris working as stall attendants to welcome the visitors.

The trade fair was also a kind of mela. Till late at night, hotel bars and ballrooms were jam-packed with foreign visitors and young Polish girls entertaining the guests. The oldest profession was then flourishing in Poland and the fair attracted members of this profession from Warsaw and other towns as well. They were a familiar sight at the hotel bars in Warsaw and the same faces were now visible in Poznan too. I was told that the only difference was that in Warsaw they quoted their fees in dollars but in Poznan the legal tender was Deutschmark since the West Germans were the foremost clients. A young German business executive who told me that every time he went out with a Polish girl, he was a gainer of 30 Deutschmark since her counterpart in Germany would charge 50 Marks as against her fee of only twenty. I also learnt that though they stuck to their demand in foreign exchange, they did offer a discount to Indians for their black eyes and hair; a novelty for them. While on this subject, I recall being told by my Polish friends that there was a madam going around Warsaw in her limousine who provided charming and sophisticated young beauties to her valued clients. They compared her to the famous Madame Claude of Paris who forbade use of the word 'prostitution and client', and was patronized by kings, presidents, ministers, ambassadors and many leaders of industry during the 1960s.

Poznan had only two main hotels, Bazar and Poznaniski; a third, Mercury, was added in 1964. Besides, foreign visitors were accommodated in private houses registered with the fair authorities. The Ministry of Foreign Trade would reserve hotel rooms for the embassies. There was often utter confusion and amusing incidents of double allotments of the same room. Once, on returning late at night, I found someone sleeping in my hotel room. So I called up the protocol officer who profusely apologized and got it vacated. As there was a shortage of hotel rooms, it was common for some seasoned visitors to get rooms by bribing the hotel staff with green bucks and American cigarettes.

The Indo-Polish Shipping Agreement provided an equitable sharing of cargo. The landlocked countries of Czechoslovakia and Hungary also used the Polish port of Gdynia for their shipments abroad, including India. With only one or two sailings a month, the Shipping Corporation of India proposed to set up their office in Gdynia. Before approving, the Ministry of External Affairs called for my comments. I pointed out that there was little justification for incurring this expenditure since I could easily handle this work with some additional travel budget to visit Prague and Budapest to secure cargo for Indian ships. I could also coordinate with the agents of the Shipping Corporation of India at Hamburg. The ministry agreed to my suggestion. This enabled me to acquaint myself with our trade exchanges with Hungary and Czechoslovakia and establish contacts with those state enterprises exporting to India. I would also pay regular visits to Gdynia to monitor the cargo shipments whenever the Shipping Corporation's vessels called there.

Air India had their offline office in Warsaw with a Polish manager, S. Rochowicz. He was quite active and frequently sought my help to get business for Air India from Polish trading enterprises. In November 1963, the Polish vice minister with a ten-member delegation was visiting Delhi for the annual trade talks. I was also summoned to Delhi for the bilateral meeting. The vice minister was going to India for the first time and I told the Polish officer at the India desk, Stalinski, that it would be a good gesture if the minister and his delegation arrived in Delhi by Air India. He promised to do it but asked me to organize a sightseeing trip to Khajuraho for the delegation. I agreed to do so without consulting anyone in the hope that our commerce ministry would endorse this deal, which they did. The Polish delegation took the

Air India flight from Prague and during their stay in India, an Indian Airlines plane was chartered to take them to Khajuraho in the morning and return in the evening. All of them, including the Polish ambassador in India, who joined the delegation, thoroughly enjoyed the trip. This also facilitated smooth sailing in negotiations for the annual trade protocol.

I found Polish society a strange mix of people with aristocratic manners holding ordinary official posts and some senior officials of state enterprises lacking gentlemanly qualities. There were many jokes about this new class of senior executives in state enterprises who got their high-ranking position through party support. The common folk were critical of the communist regime, using typical Polish humour loaded with satire to make their point. Some old, wealthy Polish families had been dispossessed of their palatial houses and allotted only a part of their own houses to live in. I met the family of one pre-war industrialist who had only two rooms for themselves in their vast villa. Apart from a bronze statue of one of their ancestors, the room walls were almost fully covered by family portraits with gilded frames. It was interesting to study three generations of the same family and their varying attitudes towards their current living conditions.

The Polish diaspora settled in the USA and West Europe, then estimated at over ten million, were free to visit Poland. The Chamber of Commerce had even set up a special unit 'Polonia' to welcome them and provide all facilities. They were encouraged to buy apartments for their relatives or for themselves if they wished to live in Warsaw on retirement. I also encountered some American women of Polish origin visiting Warsaw in search of suitable husbands to take them back to America.

The visual and performing artists enjoyed state patronage and were assured comfortable living. I got acquainted with the renowned film director Andrzej Wajda and his equally famous and charming wife Beata Tiszkiewicz who hailed from an old Polish count's family. I was impressed by their lifestyle and luxurious apartment. One Indian film producer wanted Beata to play the lead role in his film *Seleucus's Daughter*. She was even invited to Bombay but the venture failed to take off. In pursuit of my deep interest in music and having enjoyed Polish Philharmonica concerts, I established contact with the famous Warsaw Musical Society (est. 1870). They invited me to the maiden performances of upcoming young artists. Once I even invited the members of the central board of the society for an evening of Indian music at my house which they very much appreciated. It was through them that I got introduced to Miss Irena Santor, the greatest Polish singer of those days, who became a star attraction when I invited her to my private parties for Polish guests.

The world-famous Mazowsze group, with its stunning singers and dancers, was hot news whenever they gave a performance in Warsaw. I was enchanted by their song and dance and managed to visit their studios at Karolin. I invited some of their performers to my place a few times and got friendly with their vocalist Mr Babula and his teammates, Radmila and Danuta. The Mazowsze ensemble spent nearly half the year travelling abroad. They had a vast fan following all over Poland. I was once in Katovitse with the MMTC delegation led by Chairman Govind Narain. We were negotiating an iron ore export contract with Centrozap, the Polish buyers. We had invited them for dinner at the hotel restaurant and it was past eleven when the Mazowsze group came there after their performance. The moment they spotted me, Babula along with Radmila and Danuta came to greet me. I invited them to join us. The presence of the Mazowsze beauties thrilled our Polish guests and the party continued past midnight, even after our delegation had retired on my persuasion. Toasting one another's health, they enjoyed telling us about their recent London trip. Before dispersing, I sorted out a few pending issues relating to our iron ore contract with the Centrozap director. He was thrilled with the presence of the Mazowsze beauties and he admitted that it was the first time he saw them at such close quarters. Next morning at our meeting with Centrozap, they informed Mr Govind Narain that there was nothing more for negotiation since all pending issues had been settled and they had arranged a sightseeing tour for our delegation.

With my interest in art and culture I got acquainted with Mrs Suzie Hoffman, one of the most eminent painters of Poland. She had won the Lenin Award for her series of paintings on different stages of steel making. The process had even damaged her eyesight. Her monumental work had been exhibited all over East Europe. A Romanian by birth, she was married to a Polish journalist and lived in a comfortable apartment. She was fond of Indian handicrafts and old silver jewellery and also enjoyed spicy Indian food. After more than a year's association with us, she made portraits of my wife and me with a few sittings at her home studio. I vividly remember how she made me sip cognac along with coffee to bring out facial expressions of her choice. Sometime later, she told me about her project of making a series of paintings of persons in different walks of life and that she had chosen me for a diplomat. She invited me for a few sittings and repeated the drill. On our farewell, she presented an exquisite painting of flowers in a vase which still adorns the wall of my living room along with our portraits; well preserved for over fifty years.

Coming now to the Polish intelligence and spy network of the interior ministry, they kept a track of diplomats and their Polish contacts. They had officially sponsored friendship societies including one with India. The Indo-Polish Friendship Society was provided premises for holding cultural events. It was a meeting place of Indian embassy families and students to interact with

Polish men and women interested in India. The interior ministry engaged some English-speaking people in different professions. These people were encouraged to socialize with foreigners and gather their impressions of the economic and social scene in Poland. India was considered a friendly country and they were interested only in knowing through us the comments of diplomats from Western countries. I discovered this when once at Poznan two gentlemen from the interior ministry requested me to tell them about my experiences in Warsaw where they knew I had spent nearly three years and made quite a few friends. It was late at night after dinner but still I invited them to my hotel room for a chat. They asked me what Western diplomats spoke about Poland and Gomulka's regime. Instead of saying anything, I offered drinks and engaged them in a discussion about Polish music and famous singers. The meeting carried on till past midnight and they were in a jovial mood; talking about everything except the purpose of their meeting me. They left after thanking me for an enjoyable meeting. After more than a month, one of them called me up and wanted to meet me again. I gave him my address and invited him to come over. After a few days I got a call from him that it would not be possible for him to come to my house and requested me not to mention about their contacting me to any official. I stayed on in Warsaw for another six months but never heard anything from them. Later I gathered from my Polish friends that they were only doing their duty.

Another interesting case was revealed to me by a Polish lady, Mrs Irena, who perchance met me in the USA when I was posted there in 1979. She used to be a frequent guest at the Indian embassy functions in Warsaw and was also engaged every year at our pavilion in the Poznan fair to supervise the team of stall attendants and act as an interpreter. She had managed to get quite friendly with the ambassador, L.R.S. Singh, who after retirement in 1966 even invited her to India as his guest. Later, Irena married an American and migrated to the USA. Our meeting there was a strange coincidence. As consul general in Chicago, I had once invited some business figures dealing with India. Irena, then working in Houston, saw my invitation card addressed to her boss. I was surprised when she called up to greet me after more than a decade. Later, I met her at Houston. She told me that during those days in Warsaw, she had been summoned by the Intelligence Agency to inform them about her contacts with the Indian embassy and other diplomats. She was even asked to work for them but she declined.

The most extraordinary and historic case which throws light on the working of the Polish security apparatus and spy network is that of author-scholar Dr Peter Raina, an acknowledged authority on the history of Poland, renowned for his monumental biography of Cardinal Wyczinski. Dr Raina was a research scholar in Warsaw University during my time there. Owing to his proximity with Polish dissident groups, he was forced to leave Warsaw in 1967. His Polish fiancée Barbara was permitted to visit West Berlin in 1968 and get married to Dr Raina. Later, after the collapse of communism, the new Polish government's investigation into the interior ministry's activities during the communist regime revealed that Barbara was allowed to marry after she agreed to work for the ministry. She spied on her husband till 1982, when she died under mysterious circumstances. She would report his writings and meetings with Polish writers and activists in exile to the Polish Security Agency. Under the new regime, Dr Raina's outstanding contribution in recording liberal opposition movements was widely recognized. He was honoured by the Polish academic institutions. So much so, that in 2008 the Polish television even produced a documentary on Dr Raina's life.

In view of the language constraint and constant fear of being watched, the diplomats had an active social life among themselves. The British embassy had their Pink Club with a bar where diplomats and even the non-diplomatic staff of Commonwealth countries were welcome. They organized weekly tambola meetings, a popular event. There was also the British Country Club outside the city, a beautiful place with tall trees and greenery around the River Vistula. On weekends, many of us would go there for lunch and enjoy a picnic. The American Club with its bar and cafeteria open to all diplomats was a popular meeting place. No Polish guests were allowed at these clubs. We took them to popular bars and restaurants of Europiski Hotel and Grand Hotel. The old town, destroyed during the war, was rebuilt with painstaking efforts as an exact replica of the original. It was another fascinating quarter of the city with swanky cafes offering delicious coffee and tea with appetizing snacks.

While in Warsaw, I got an opportunity to make my maiden visit to Moscow, the fountainhead of the communist bloc. It was in July 1963 that we held the first grand Indian exhibition at Moscow, the biggest trade show ever held by India abroad. Indian trade and industry were represented by over a hundred participants. A vast range of traditional and manufactured products were put on display. A great attraction for Russians was the Indian restaurant Moti Mahal, specially included in the show with its skilled chefs and paraphernalia. It offered tandoori chicken and other dishes. It was quite a sight to find hundreds of Russian men and women queuing up to taste Indian delicacies.

The director of exhibitions, P.K. Panikkar, an old friend of mine from the commerce ministry days, asked me to bring a Polish delegation to visit the Indian exhibition at Moscow and stay over to assist him in handling and coordinating important trade enquiries. I found my two-week stay highly rewarding as I was able to learn a lot about life in Moscow and the functioning of Soviet trade enterprises. This proved valuable when I was posted to Moscow. Thanks to the Russian interpreter provided to me, I was able to go around the city by public transport and witness Russians queuing up everywhere: theatres, cinemas, restaurants, wine shops, food stores, ice cream parlours, etc. Six years later, I was happy to be posted to Moscow.

Another rewarding upshot of the Moscow tour was my favourable interaction with Ambassador T.N. Kaul. He observed my canvassing for Indian export products with the Polish delegation, the only one to come from East Europe for the Indian exhibition. I had a few occasions to officially meet Mr Kaul and acquaint him with my economic background and commercial experience. He seemed to like me, and a few months later I got his message asking me to meet him at the Palace of Culture, the landmark of Warsaw, at an appointed time. He was on his way to Moscow with his new Mercedes car which he had picked up at Stuttgart. I was amazed to see him driving all by himself from Germany and reach the agreed spot at the appointed time. He stayed in Warsaw for two days and I accompanied him wherever he wished to go. This gave me an opportunity to know Mr Kaul, who was a doyen of our foreign service, better and get a feel of his lively and vigorous personality. His sense of humour and informal ways deeply impressed me. Though I never worked with him, I had many occasions to meet him in Delhi and abroad. After retirement I kept up my association with him till the end.

12

In Tito's Land

THE INDO-PAK CONFLICT OF SEPTEMBER 1965 and the ensuing economy measures held in abeyance all postings and transfers. I had to stay on at Warsaw for another six months after completing my three-year term. In April 1966, I was transferred to Belgrade as first secretary (political). Fortunately for me, a counsellor (political) also joined there against a newly created post. Our ambassador J.K. Atal, was a fine gentleman with a unique personality. He thought there was no need to have an additional officer and so he surrendered the post of the first secretary (political) and accommodated me against the post of first secretary (commercial) whose designated incumbent had not arrived yet. I was happy to continue in the commercial field and so was the commerce ministry. They took no time to confirm my posting and cancel the appointment of the selected officer. This was the first extraordinary instance of its kind where an ambassador, instead of asking for additional staff to enhance his importance, chose to surrender an officer's post. At the headquarters, the corridor gossip held me responsible for manoeuvring things in order to continue in the commercial wing of the mission.

The decade of the 1960s was the glorious period of Indo-Yugoslav ties, political and economic. As with other socialist countries of East Europe, we had similar bilateral trade and payment agreements and the non-convertible Indian rupee served as a unit of account. Trade exchanges were covered by the annual trade plans which stipulated the items of export from India with their value or quantity, and import items from Yugoslavia in the same way providing for a balanced turnover. The payment arrangement covered non-commercial transactions as well.

Indo-Yugoslav friendship, which had matured after Tito's visit to India in 1954–55, contributed a great deal to the expansion of trade and economic relations between the two countries. By the mid-1960s, India had emerged as a major trading partner of Yugoslavia among the developing countries. Bilateral trade rose from less than one million dollars in 1955 to about one hundred million dollars in 1967. This trade was also bolstered by Yugoslav credits to India involving deliveries of Yugoslav cargo ships and some other equipment.

The Yugoslav brand of socialism differed from the Soviet bloc countries. Agriculture was mostly in private hands and the industrial and commercial enterprises were autonomous under workers' self-management regime driven by profit motives. They were free to compete with one another earning rewards for greater efficiency.

Yugoslavia attracted more Indian business visitors than Poland where one had to deal with a single state enterprise for selling or buying any product. Here, there was a choice of dealing with different trading companies who worked for Indian exporters on a commission basis and assembled buyers from different parts of Yugoslavia. Inter-Trade, with its headquarters at Ljubljana in Slovenia, was the leading Yugoslav company handling trade with

India. It had its network not only in major cities of Yugoslavia like Zagreb and Belgrade but had also set up its office in Delhi as Yugo-Intraco. Most Indian exporters conducted their business operations through Yugoslav trading companies in Belgrade.

Yugoslavia then was a mosaic of different nationalities with its six republics: Serbia, Croatia, Slovenia, Macedonia, Montenegro and Bosnia-Herzegovina. The official language was Serbo-Croatian with its two scripts. With its diversity and multi-religious build-up comprising the Orthodox Church, Catholics, Protestants and even Islam, Yugoslavia with its twenty million population was known as 'miniature India'.

Both India and Yugoslavia were then keen to expand and diversify their trade through new forms of economic cooperation. A historic announcement for tripartite cooperation was made at a conference in New Delhi in October 1966 by three leaders, Mrs Indira Gandhi, Marshal Tito and President Nasser. It was resolved to join in an effort to 'expand the area of mutual cooperation, increase trade exchanges among themselves, pool technical and scientific experience and undertake joint endeavours to develop mutually beneficial patterns of trade and development'. This was followed by the establishment of three ad hoc working groups: one to negotiate tariff preferences, payment procedures, and measures for expanding trade; another to consider prospects for industrial specialization; and a third to explore the formation of a joint shipping company. I was associated with follow-up meetings held at Cairo, Belgrade and Rijeka. A notable outcome was the implementation of a Tripartite Agreement on Tariff Preferences in April 1968, covering more than 500 products and valid for five years.

Among new forms of economic cooperation, a notable deal was the export of Indian rail wagons to Hungary after their assembly in Yugoslavia. It was negotiated and finalized by the chairman of

STC, Mr B.P. Patel, and received much publicity as it signalled the entry of India in a new field of engineering export.

A major commercial event in Yugoslavia was the Zagreb international trade fair. It was a meeting point of East and West with the participation of many Western industrialized countries along with the Soviet bloc and developing ones led by India. A grand Indian exhibition held in Belgrade in 1965 had familiarized the Yugoslav people with a large variety of Indian textiles and other manufactured consumer products, especially the brands popular in the West. The Zagreb fair in East Europe turned out to be most popular with the Indian business community. To attract larger Indian participation, the Yugoslav authorities granted special permission to Indian exporters to sell their goods at the fair. Besides, these were the 'P' form days when foreign travel was restricted and participation in trade fairs a valid licence to go abroad. Yugoslavia was a tourist paradise with easy access to Italy, Austria and Germany. So many so-called participants just showed their faces on the inauguration day and vanished to other countries for pleasure. On the other hand, some exporters who brought Indian handicrafts, shawls, silk scarves, dresses, stoles, costume jewellery, etc., for sale during the fair did roaring business with huge profits. When this news spread, organizers of the Indian Council of Trade Fairs and Exhibitions, Bombay, headed by Prem Nath, were flooded with applications for participation at the Zagreb fair in 1969. I was asked to screen applicants on the basis of their business in Yugoslavia. I declined to do so and recommended that all applicants should be asked to apply through their respective export promotion councils. Prem Nath accepted this and the established exporters were equally satisfied. The Indian pavilion used to be a star attraction at the fair and President Tito invariably graced it with a visit. He would be welcomed by Ambassador J.K. Atal, who was quite intimate with him, having accompanied him on riding and hunting excursions.

Another notable and delightful business event was the Indian fashion show at the Belgrade Textile Fair in 1968. The Indian Handloom Export Promotion Council participating in the fair had asked me to organize the show. With a limited budget it was not possible to entrust the job to a Yugoslav agency on a turnkey basis. So I engaged a dress designer, selected four models and got the dresses of handloom cotton and silk materials tailored to their sizes. India was the only foreign participant to present such a colourful show to promote its exports of handloom textiles. Beautiful and charming, the Yugoslav models, adorned with glittering Indian handcrafted costume jewellery and attired in designer dresses, presented a colourful show every evening for five days. The fashion show, a novel experiment, was quite fruitful businesswise.

During 1968, an Indian trade exhibition was organized at Prague which attracted business visitors from other East European countries. I was invited, along with other commercial secretaries from our embassies in East Europe, to attend the exhibition. It gave me an opportunity to meet officials of the Czechoslav trade enterprises dealing with India. This has remained a memorable visit since I was lucky to fly out of Prague by the last flight before the airport was closed with Soviet forces marching in to overturn the Dubcek regime, a revolutionary event in East Europe.

We were making strenuous efforts to diversify our trade with Yugoslavia through exports of our newly developed engineering and machine tool industry. After their success in Bulgaria, the Tatas were keen to export their trucks to Yugoslavia. Indian manufactures of hand tools, automobile components, sanitary fittings and wire ropes after participating at Zagreb fair succeeded in introducing their products in the Yugoslav market. The most significant case was that of Mahindra jeeps. Their director and export manager made several visits to Belgrade when they were extended full support and help in negotiations with the Yugoslav government. So much so, that finally we sought the intervention of the Yugoslav foreign trade minister. Ultimately the deal was reportedly approved by President Tito himself and Mahindras got an order for export of 2,000 jeeps to Yugoslavia. It was hailed as a historic achievement for the Indian industry to make this inroad in Europe.

In view of the close Indo-Yugoslav close ties, there was regular exchange of delegations led by ministers. Even Prime Minister Indira Gandhi visited Belgrade in 1968 and met President Tito at his palace on the island of Brioni in the Adriatic Sea. It was Tito's favourite home which had become a place of international pilgrimage. It was here that Nehru and Nasser joined Tito in 1956 to proclaim the role of non-alignment in the world of power blocs. I had an opportunity to visit Brioni when Ambassador J.K. Atal presented his credentials to President Tito in 1966. The only non-official Indian received by President Tito was the leading Indian industrialist G.D. Birla, who had earlier met both the American and Russian heads of governments. It was at our ambassador's intervention with the Yugoslav foreign minister that this meeting was arranged. Other notable visits were by our ministers Manubhai Shah, Dinesh Singh and V.K.R.V. Rao. The Indian export promotion councils also did not lag behind and sent their delegations to explore and promote exports. Around this time a new trade body NAYE (National Alliance of Young Entrepreneurs) was instituted in Delhi. They also brought a big delegation representing leading industrial houses to establish contact with Yugoslav enterprises. Two Indian business houses, viz., the Ruia Group of Bombay and Tractors and Farm Equipment (TAFE) of Madras had even set up their offices in Belgrade. Their representatives Ashok Kumar and Ved Ahuja were not only active in Yugoslavia but also spread their wings to other East European countries.

Coming to some interesting episodes of Indian delegations I recall one of N.R. Reddy, joint secretary, Ministry of Finance hosting a reception at Metropol Hotel, Belgrade after the signing of the Yugoslav credit agreement. He spent a good amount of his personal funds to entertain Yugoslav guests, even presenting bouquets of flowers to all the ladies present at the reception. He was fond of drinks and often got inebriated but everyone laughed it out including the foreign trade minister, Manubhai Shah. Reddy would joke that his name stood for 'Never Reddy'. He was quite informal with the minister and told me not to bother about him since he was clever enough to find ways and means to entertain himself. I was greatly impressed by Reddy's genius when he dictated the draft agreement from memory as the relevant file was misplaced in transit. Another interesting episode relates to the visit of our shipping minister, V.K.R.V. Rao. He was scheduled to arrive at Belgrade in the morning and I was to accompany him to the port of Rijeka by a domestic flight. He missed his flight at Frankfurt and came by an evening flight. This coincided with Prime Minister Indira Gandhi's visit to Yugoslavia. Rao wanted to stay over in Belgrade for the night and meet Mrs Gandhi. She declined to meet him and the Yugoslav government arranged a special train to take us to Rijeka same night.

One VIP who impressed me as a polite and modest gentleman was the deputy minister of commerce, Chowdhary Ram Sevak. He was invited by the Yugoslav government to visit the Zagreb international trade fair in 1969. We had a small reception for him at the Indian pavilion and he was glad to meet our businessmen. All of us enjoyed drinks but Ram Sevak did not take alcohol. Later, when I went to leave him at the hotel, he told me that he would like to take some cognac on health grounds. It took me a little time to make him shed his hesitation and he became quite friendly with me and even enjoyed our staple drink Scotch and soda. The Bulgarian government had also invited him to visit the Plovdiv fair which was held soon after the Zagreb fair. So, Ram Sevak came to Belgrade for a day and was to fly to Sofia. He asked me if I could arrange his travel to Sofia by road as he would like to see the countryside. On my part the STC had asked me to visit Plovdiv fair and handle some specific trade deals. So, I took him to Sofia in my car and told the Bulgarian hosts to receive us in front of Hotel Balkan at a specified time. It was a pleasant drive and the countryside in golden autumn presented a delightful sight. Bulgaria was then hailed as the granary of the Soviet bloc and a major exporter of fruits and vegetables to West Europe. As we reached before time, we took a round of the city and arrived at the hotel at the appointed time. There I handed over the deputy minister to the charge of our embassy's first secretary, K.K. Bhargava, who was present there with the Bulgarian hosts to welcome us.

Another VIP of eminence to visit Belgrade was the leading industrialist G.D. Birla, then hailed as the 'aluminium king of India' with his cherished Hindalco exporting aluminium to Europe. I accompanied him to his meeting with the president of Energoinvest, Mr Blum, a leading business figure of Yugoslavia. It was about a joint venture for an aluminium plant in Yugoslavia. For me it was quite educative to listen to G.D. Birla discussing the proposal without any file or paper. He had full mastery of the minutest details of the project. I vividly remember Birla asserting that he did not conceive any business without profit, which should be the driving force for a successful businessman. Considering the cost of electric energy in Yugoslavia, he pointed out that an aluminium project was not feasible since electric power was the vital component of aluminium production. So, he suggested the setting up of a captive power plant for the project. Anyway, their negotiations continued with a follow-up visit of Blum to Calcutta.

In the field of cultural exchange, we had visits from Bharatanatyam dancer Yamini Krishnamurthy, and Ravi Shankar. The latter had already earned name and fame in the West and had little knowledge about the socialist countries of East Europe. Besides, his teaming up with the Beatles and consequent publicity had made him egotistic and pompous. As I was asked to handle the visit, I managed to collect a small respectable audience for his performance. Ravi Shankar told me in a haughty tone that the audience was too small. I reminded him that he was on a cultural exchange visit and if he cared so much about the audience and not his performing art, he should have told the government before coming. He kept quiet and gave a lukewarm performance; and so was the applause.

Yugoslav popular music and songs had an oriental tinge and I found them quite pleasing. Their Kolo dance and music drove everyonc to join the hilarious merriment and fun. Their favourite drink was plum brandy and red wine. They brewed wine at home as we make pickles. Yugoslavs also liked popular Indian film music as they had seen Indian movies dubbed in Russian. The Writers' Club in Belgrade was my favourite haunt where one could enjoy delicious Serbian dishes with red wine. After the conclusion of ballet and theatre shows, the singers, dancers, actors and playwrights flocked to this place. It was here that I met a number of artists including the famous singer Lola Novakovich, ballerina Atanasova, and actor Ristanovich. There was live music at every good restaurant and often a talented singer would attract more customers than the cuisine. There were also violinists who would come to your table and play to entertain you and earn their tips. They would rush to attend on their regular patrons and would even

Pt Barkat Ram (Father) who taught me there is no substitute for hard work and no short-cut to success.

Smt. Puran Devi (Mother) who instilled in me the love for music.

Lawrence and Montgomery Halls in Lawrence Gardens, Lahore, 1920. (Courtesy British Library, London)

Government College, the most prestigious college in Lahore. Only highly meritorious students could hope to join it though scions of landlords, title-holders and high-ranking government officials were given preference, 1940.

DAV High School (now Islamia), was founded in memory of Swami Dayanand Saraswati, the founder of Arya Samaj. The school laid emphasis on bramacharya (celibacy) and moral character, Lahore, 1997.

I as first year college student, 1937.

In front of my house at Nisbet Road, Lahore, 1942.

My friends and I (centre) at our convocation at the University of Punjab, Lahore, 1943.

Trudging through snow on my trip to Amarnath Cave, Kashmir, 1939.

My college friends and I (lying) at Juhu beach on a trip sponsored by the University of Punjab, Bombay, 1941.

My wife Savitri and I after our ceremonial marriage, Lahore, 1947. We eloped and had a civil marriage in January, and a month later performed a ceremonial wedding at the insistence of our families.

I (centre) was seen off by my kith and kin at Delhi Railway Station for my departure to Tokyo, 1956.

Nargita, a Romanian singer of Hindi film songs calling on Prime Minister Indira Gandhi, 1968.

Beata Tiszkiewicz, leading lady of Polish cinema, Warsaw, 1966.

Tamancha Jan, renowned singer of Lahore, 1944.

My wife and I (extreme right) with Ambassador C.S. Jha and Mrs Jha, Tokyo, 1956.

My interpreter, assigned to me for my visit to India's grand trade exhibition, and I at the Red Square, Moscow, 1963.

Farewell to Ambassador L.R.S. Singh (centre) at the Indian Embassy Warsaw, 1964.

At the Indian pavilion,
Pozman International Fair, 1963.

G. D. Birla (centre) and I (third from left) at Sarajevo, Yugoslavia, 1969.

President Tito of Yugoslavia, one of the founders of the Non-Aligned Movement and who worked closely with Pt Jawahar Lal Nehru, at the Indian pavilion, Zagreb International Trade Fair, 1968.

With the Mayor of Chicago, M.A. Bilandic, 1977.

Chairing the UNCTAD seminar; I served as an advisor on trade and economic relations with socialist countries of East Europe, Sofia, 1983.

I acted as a priest at Miss Kumar's marriage ceremony, Geneva, 1983. The entire wedding party had arrived but there was no trace of the Brahmin priest who was to fly from London. The bride's side knew that I was a Brahmin, with a working knowledge of Sanskrit, and requested me to perform the ceremony.

At an American wedding, Boston, 1994.

Anarkali Bazar, Lahore, 1997.

Revisited my house at Lahore, 1997.

Dingha Singh Building, landmark of Mall Road, Lahore, 1997.

My lifelong friend Saeed Ahmed Khan and I, Lahore, 1999.

Haji Fazal Kareem, the only Muslim student at DAV High School, and I, Lahore, 1999

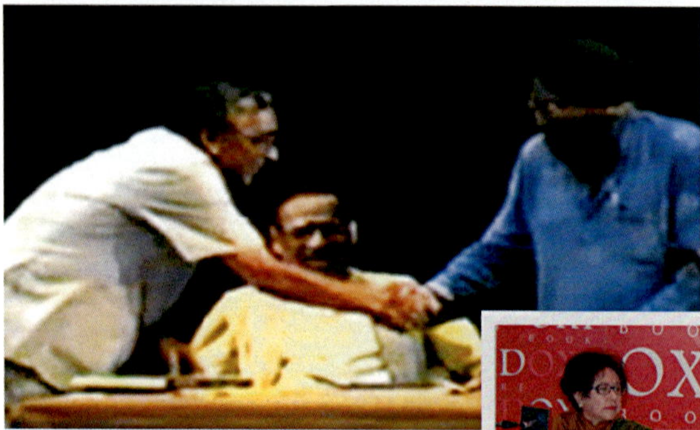

Vasant Sathe and Khushwant Singh launch my book, *Nautch Girls of India,* 1996.

Pakistan High Commissioner Aziz Ahmad Khan and I (right) at the launch of the book *Lahore- City of Sin and Splendour,* by the famous writer Bapsi Sidhwa, Delhi, 2004.

Natwar Singh, former Union cabinet minister, at the launch of *Raj Revisted,* authored by me (left), New Delhi, 2012.

Madeeha Gauhar (left), theatre personality, Feryal Gauhar, eminent film-maker and novelist of Pakistan, and me, Lahore, 2013.

The members of the Lahore Club and I at the India International Centre, 1995.

The renowned author of *My Feudal Lord,* Tehmima Durrani, and I at the Lahore Literary Festival, 2014.

Penny Thomson (second from left), an English lady who wanted to trace her grandfather, Inder Singh of Lahore, approached me for the task. Her Indian family with me (centre), Delhi, 1999.

The students of Government College
of Lahore and I (centre), Lahore, 2014.

The author's portrait, 2015.

play popular Indian film tunes, especially those from Raj Kapoor's *Awara*, which had made a mark all over East Europe.

It would be apt to make a mention here of Nargita, a Romanian singer of Hindi film songs known to the Air India manager, Ranvir Tiwari, who was impressed after hearing her in Bucharest. On his persuasion I invited her to Belgrade and organized her concert at our ambassador's residence. Young and charming, dressed in a saree with costume jewellery, she enraptured the audience with her seductive appearance, melodious voice and filmy dance. The managing director of HMV, Bhaskar Menon, who happened to be present there, invited her to India. Mr Tiwari offered her a complimentary return air ticket. On my part I asked some of my friends to take care of her in Delhi. For Nargita it was her dream come true. She had a gala time for two weeks in India and even called on Prime Minister Indira Gandhi. Almost a decade later, I met her in Bucharest and learnt she hailed from the gypsy community, which is said to have old Indian links. Nargita was adopted name. She told me that her favourite stars were Nargis and Geeta Bali and so she combined the two names and made her name 'Nargita'.

My tenure in Belgrade turned out to be all the more happy and enjoyable since both other colleagues, viz., Military Attache Col. Y.P. Sethi and First Secretary (Information) Jagmohan Mahajan happened to be my friends and classmates from Government College, Lahore. Ambassador J.K. Atal used to laugh at this rare and strange coincidence and called us a gang of three. Counsellor (Political) Mr Prithvi Singh, imposed on the embassy by the ministry without the ambassador's consent, felt uncomfortable with the three of us. The Indian community in Belgrade was limited to business representatives Ashok Kumar and V.P. Ahuja, mentioned earlier, the PTI representative R. Chary and Air India manager Ranvir Tiwari. A fine gentleman, Yousuf from Air India endeared himself to one and all who came into his contact. I struck a lifelong friendship with him. Hailing from South Africa, Yousuf, with his liberal education in England, felt suffocated during those apartheid days. So, he came to Bombay and joined Air India. Unfortunately, he passed away in Dacca in 1979, soon after his retirement.

Our Embassy in Belgrade also covered Greece, where we had only a Greek honorary council, L.E. Vafiadis, who had spent several years in India with a Greek company Rallis-India. I used to visit Athens once every quarter to meet their trade ministry officials and some leading Greek business houses to explore the prospects of promoting trade.

Towards the end of 1968 a memorable incident of grief and relief cropped up in my official career. The Ministry of External Affairs came out with a list of Grade-I IFS (B) officers approved for promotion to the senior scale of IFS (A). In spite of my seniority and commendable work record I was left out. It was a rude shock for me since I had received several letters of appreciation for my work from the commerce ministry. It turned out that K.B. Lal, the then commerce secretary and member of the Foreign Service Board, could not attend the board meeting when the promotion list was finalized. He had already got me selected for posting to Tokyo to handle Indian participation at the Osaka World Expo, 1970. This was a plum posting but I was depressed for not getting my due promotion. However, as luck would have it, within the same week I received a message from the Foreign Office asking me if I would accept posting to Moscow as the STC's chief for East Europe-cum-commercial adviser in the Indian embassy with the rank and salary of a counsellor, one step higher than the IFS senior scale.

Earlier I had prepared a note on the STC's business operations in the socialist countries of East Europe and the change in functioning offices. I had suggested turning the Moscow office into a regional hub for supervising and coordinating the activities of these offices in East Europe. I had sent this note to my friend S. Ramachandran, formerly joint secretary, Ministry of Commerce and now director in the STC. He recommended my scheme to the chairman, Prakash Tandon, who was equally impressed with the proposal. I had informed them about the Soviet trade representatives' close association with commercial counsellors of the East European countries stationed in Delhi. My proposal had found favour with K.B. Lal as well. So when the STC chairman was on the lookout for a suitable person for Moscow, his choice fell upon me. Ambassador Atal asked me if I would forego my plum posting to Tokyo and go to Moscow. He was somewhat surprised at my nod for Moscow. Finally I got the official appointment in Moscow and was asked to join there as soon as possible.

Returning to the case of my promotion, it is strange and amusing to find that the Ministry of External Affairs did not find me up to the mark for promotion to the IFS senior scale, Rs 900–1,800. On the other hand, the Ministry of Commerce found me deserving enough to be appointed as the STC's chief at Moscow in the scale of Rs 1,800–2,200. It was perhaps the only case of its kind in the annals of Government of India service.

13

Athens and Cairo: From Sirtaki to Belly Dance

MY CONCURRENT ACCREDITATION TO GREECE MADE my Belgrade posting all the more interesting and enjoyable. Our honorary consul at Athens, L.E. Vafiadis, looked after the issuance of visas but received some trade enquiries also which he passed on to me. I found the Greek businessmen friendly. They invariably talked about their old historic ties with India, dating from the time of Alexander the Great, that is, the fourth century BC. I tried to introduce some Indian-manufactured products which were competitive both in quality and price, especially those required in their ships. Greece was then one of the leading nations in merchant shipping. The wealthy ship-owning families dominated the social and cultural life of Athens. Indian businessmen had negligible contact with the Greek market. So, I brought in the STC and advised their manager visiting Belgrade to go to Athens and meet prospective Greek importers. After a couple of successful deals, I persuaded the STC to appoint our honorary consul Vafiadis as their representative on regular commission basis.

I also went to Athens to assist the visiting government delegations. The most notable event in Athens was the International Symposium on Industrial Development held by the United Nations International Development (UNIDO) in December 1967. The Indian delegation was led by the then industry secretary, N.N. Wanchoo, ICS, and included P.C. Alexander and K.J. George, joint secretaries. Business leaders from Indian industry included S.L. Kirloskar and M.M. Ruia. UNIDO was then headed by I.H. Abdel Rahman from Egypt. The Indian delegation raised the issue of encouraging investments in developing countries, which was much applauded. The Symposium laid the foundation of UNIDO's comprehensive programme of future activities in cooperation with other UN Agencies.

An enjoyable part of the Symposium was a trip to Crete Island organized by the Greek authorities hosting the event. S.L. Kirloskar hosted a reception for the official delegation. This was an occasion where Kirloskar sought my help for some of their pending business deals in Belgrade. Mr Ruia, who was also present, offered the services of his Belgrade office to Kirloskar, who agreed to take his help. That is how Kirloskars' Cummings engines were marketed in Yugoslavia. I recall an amusing episode when Mr Ruia invited Indian delegation leader Mr Wanchoo to a nightclub and told me to join him much to the discomfiture of Mr Wanchoo who, conscious of his ICS label, considered me too junior to sit with him and that too at a nightclub. Mr Ruia knew me well, having met me quite a few times on his visits to Belgrade.

Coming to the social and cultural scene, Athens during the 1960s was a tourists' paradise. The Hollywood classic *Zorba the Greek* (1964) had generated worldwide interest and popularity for the Greek dance 'sirtaki' and 'bouzouki music'. The big mandolin-like instrument bouzouki with its exciting strains became famous during this period. The music of Greece is as diverse and celebrated as its history. Sirtaki is a popular dance of Greek origin. It was in fact created in 1964 for *Zorba the Greek* from the mixture of slow and fast versions of the Hasapiko dance and was choreographed by Giorgos Provias. Then Athony Quinn, the film's hero, in his historic role offered a rare glimpse of the glorious dance and immortalized both the music and the dance as well as the composer, Mikis Theodorakis. *Zorba the Greek* brought more tourists to Greece during the 1960's than any other campaign by the National Tourist Organization. Personally, I was enchanted by Greek music and lyrics even without understanding the words. I was captivated by famous singers of the time like Nana Mouskouri and Poly Panou, who had attained worldwide fame.

Thanks to Mr Vafiadis, our honorary consul, I was able to visit several entertainment spots in the famous Plaka area. Plaka is not only a tourist hub of Athens but one of the oldest towns in the world, cluttered around the northern and eastern slopes of the Acropolis. The taverns there beckon you with the sound of music from evening to well past midnight. Once a Greek friend of mine took me to a popular Greek restaurant in downtown Athens where I saw people turning up only after 10 p.m. It was a memorable experience with wine and music casting their magical spell. The Greek dancers in their colourful traditional costumes and headgear presented a marvellous sight. The enchanting strains of bouzouki drove us to drink generously from our wine cups. Then I witnessed an amazing scene of revellers tossing and smashing their wine cups on the floor. The tinkling sound of breaking glass added further gusto to the merriment. I also saw the simultaneous cleaning operation of broken glass pieces to make way for fresh onslaughts by the pleasure seekers. The whole ambience was so charged with glee and hilarity that I saw some American tourists getting up and dancing to the sound of music especially when they played the sirtaki air from *Zorba the Greek*. My host went on repeating his orders for wine and new glass cups. For me, it was an unforgettable treat. Later, I learnt that at times the restaurant bill for breaking glassware for fun exceeded that for food and drinks.

Those were the days when one rarely encountered Indian tourists in Athens. Our honorary consul, a successful businessman, had influential contacts in Athens. He would take me to his parties and introduce me to his friends who were interested in knowing more about India and its people. I remember meeting a wealthy lady, Laura Pandos, who enjoyed entertaining foreign diplomats. She was so generous that once after a late dinner party at her house she asked me to take one of her cars and not call for a cab. Then she insisted that I should keep the car with me during my stay in Athens. She had never visited India but was interested in everything Indian.

Hotel Galaxy in the city centre was my favourite place of stay in Athens. Mr Vafiadis was friendly with the hotel owner and introduced me to him on my first visit. I began to be treated as a special guest and even after an escalation of the hotel's tariffs I was charged the old rate. A major trade event in Greece was the annual International Trade Fair at Salonika. The Greek Chamber of Commerce was keen about Indian participation but unfortunately I could not succeed in organizing that during my stay.

Now I come to Cairo, the city of pyramids and home to the ancient Egyptian civilization. I first visited Cairo in 1962 while travelling to Europe by sea. It was a day trip with a conducted tour for passengers as the ship passed through the Suez Canal. We had got down at Port Said and joined the ship in the evening at Alexandria. It was hot and humid but visiting the Pyramids at Giza was a true delight.

The tripartite conference held in New Delhi in October 1966 by the leaders of India, the UAR and Yugoslavia while reaffirming their commitment to non-alignment had resolved to undertake concrete measures to expand mutual trade and economic cooperation. The first meeting of the tripartite working group was held in Cairo in January 1967. I was summoned to join the Indian delegation for this meeting. Apart from participating in trade discussions and working out a tariff preferential arrangement, the visit to Cairo was indeed an enjoyable experience. As state guests we were lodged at the historic Shepherds Hotel, famous for having hosted the Prime Minister Winston Churchill. As generous hosts the Egyptians took care to arrange delightful sightseeing tours to their historic sites and boat rides in the Nile. Then there were lavish receptions by different government bodies.

The 'Son et Lumiere' show at the Pyramids and Sphinx was a memorable experience. The harmonious play of light and music with delightful commentary presented a majestic, unforgettable spectacle of glorious monuments, heralding the dawn of history. We also heard the mellifluous voice of Oum Kalsoum, then the greatest singing voice of the Arab world. The evening's highlight was watching the original belly dance by the renowned performer Nahed Sabri, famous for her enchanting dance in the movie, *A Thousand and One Nights* (1964). Having seen only fake belly dance numbers in Hollywood movies, Nahed Sabri's performance was sheer delight and we were mesmerized by the sound of lutes and drums dictating the dancer's swinging tempo.

I got another opportunity to visit Cairo in 1969 at the Tripartite Conference of Foreign Trade Ministers of India, UAR and Yugoslavia. The Indian minister B.R. Bhagat could not come for the inaugural session and was represented by Secretary K.B. Lal. He informed the Egyptian hosts that some pressing state matters had compelled the minister to delay his visit and he would join before the concluding session. Officials of the three delegations carried on discussions on the set agenda and worked out agreed drafts of tripartite agreements for expansion and diversification of trade and economic cooperation. My job was to interact with Yugoslavian officials and evolve a common approach on different issues coming up for discussions. As regards drafting of documents, the Indian delegation played a leading role and I assisted them in this task. I also acted an an aide to K.B. Lal who wanted me to be with him during his special meetings with leaders of the Yugoslav and UAR delegations. He would ask me to join him in the evenings as well when he entertained some VIPs. He jokingly told our delegation members that being a diplomat, I was a fit person to take care of his foreign guests. Once while I was so engaged, a senior member of the Indian delegation dropped in and requested Mr Lal to relieve me for assisting them in some discussion. Mr Lal politely dismissed him pointing out that I was doing more important official work. Throughout my long association with Mr Lal I always looked up to him not only as a great boss but also as my guru in all respects. The Conference work was nearly complete and we were waiting for the minister for final signing of the documents at the concluding session. I was with K.B. Lal when the minister called up from Delhi and asked him when he should come. Mr Lal told him that the Conference had completed its deliberations and Indian proposals had been agreed to. He added that the concluding session of ministers was a mere formality and he need not take the trouble of coming all the way if he was otherwise busy. That is how the Indian minister stayed away and K.B. Lal played the minister's role at the concluding session.

While in Cairo this time I had an opportunity to meet Ambassador Apa Saheb Pant, held in great esteem in our service circles. He invited me for dinner and had an interesting discussion about the trade and economy of the socialist countries of East Europe, especially Yugoslavia. He was keen to know about the Yugoslav brand of socialism and its economic relations with the Soviet Union. I invited him to make a private visit to Yugoslavia, which he did a few months later. His knowledge and experience and his interest in knowing more about the socialist world impressed me a great deal.

As regards the sightseeing programme, we were taken this time to Luxor where we were amazed to see the ancient Egyptian architecture. I was wonder-struck by the remains of temples and tombs and massive sculptures in the Valley of the Kings. This time we were lodged at the Nile Hilton with its modern five-star luxury and a nightclub. It was there that I had the good luck of watching the enchanting performance of Soheir Zaki, hailed as the queen of belly dance in Egypt. In the 1960s she had received awards from the Shah of Iran, the Tunisian president and Gamal Abdel Nasser. Soheir Zaki was called the Oum Kalsoum of dance. While Oum sang with her voice, Soheir sang with her body. It was indeed a rare treat to witness the live performance of the greatest belly dancer of her times and a national icon of Egypt.

My visits to Athens and Cairo remain permanently embedded in my memory as I could not repeat them.

14

Moscow: Commercial Adviser and STC Chief for East Europe

I JOINED DUTIES IN MOSCOW ON 22 October 1969, my birthday. The State Trading Corporation's office was part of the Indian embassy in line with the practice followed by Soviet state enterprises whose representatives were members of the trade wing of their embassy. No private Indian business house was allowed to open an office in Moscow. Indian businessmen could visit Moscow only after their meetings with the Soviet enterprises concerned had been approved by the trade representation in India. The STC's office in Moscow provided assistance to Indian exporters who chose to associate with it. Besides, it handled the imports on government account and exports of items canalized through the STC.

The STC had a large showroom on Lomonosovsky Prospect for the display of Indian export products where officials of the trade enterprises concerned were invited to negotiate business deals. The showroom, opened in 1965, had served its purpose and was now lying in disuse. Our embassy was then facing an acute shortage of space due to expansion of its defence wing. I recommended to Ambassador D.P. Dhar to wind up the showroom and shift STC's office there, to which he readily agreed. I converted the showroom into an office with enough space for the staff and storage of samples. A section of the premises was set apart for an ad hoc display of specific products when required. Incidentally, this shifting was most welcome for me since apart from having an independent set-up away from the embassy, I was close to my residence that was on the seventh floor of the same building. Technically, a part of Indian embassy, STC's office had its own separate budget, though accounts were managed by the embassy. I was provided with adequate funds to visit and supervise the functioning of branch offices in Berlin, Prague, Budapest and Belgrade. As regards other socialist countries of East Europe, viz., Poland, Bulgaria and Romania, I handled STC's trading operations with them from Moscow and travelled there from time to time as required. Those were glorious days of India's economic ties with Soviet bloc countries. We had long-term trade and payments agreements with them and concluded annual trade plans containing lists of export and import items along with their value or volume. The STC played an important role in trade negotiations with these countries.

On my part, with over seven years of experience of working in East Europe, and well conversant with the working of foreign trade regimes there, I came to be considered as an expert by the Ministry of Commerce. So, I was thrilled when soon after my taking over at Moscow I was called upon by the ministry to go to Belgrade and assist the Indian trade delegation visiting there. Yugoslavia was reluctant to renew the bilateral Rupee Payment Agreement and wanted to change over to free foreign exchange. It had amassed considerable foreign exchange reserves through booming tourism and remittances from Yugoslav workers abroad. They were aiming to make the dinar convertible and wanted to discontinue their clearing account trade exchanges with old partners. On our side, we were apprehensive that discontinuance of the rupee trade with Yugoslavia would set a bad precedent that might affect our Rupee Payment Agreements with other countries. It was after long-drawn-out discussions and political intervention that Yugoslavia finally agreed to extend the Rupee Payment Agreement for another two years. At the same time it was decided to set up a branch office of the STC in Belgrade. Within the next three months, all formalities were completed, accommodation arranged and STC's office as part of the embassy was set up in Belgrade with Mr Vidyasagar as branch manager.

After an introductory three-month spell in Moscow, I came to Delhi for a two-week briefing at the STC's headquarters. The most educative was my meeting with Chairman Prakash Tandon, the management guru of his time and former first Indian chairman of Hindustan Lever. He had reorganized the functioning of STC as a corporate body. His team comprised Vice Chairman P.J. Fernandes and three directors, M.C. Sareen, H.R. Bhalla and Dr V. Nath. He encouraged them to take decisions and not run to the ministry for orders. The managers were instructed to discard the bureaucratic way of working and adopt business-like modus operandi. As for me, I got acquainted with STC's directors and senior managers and learnt about the activities of different divisions and their trading operations with the state foreign trade enterprises of the Soviet Union and other countries of East Europe. The two divisions most active in the Soviet market were leather and knitwear. The entire export of leather footwear and woollen knitwear to the Soviet Union was routed through the STC, which maintained a panel of approved manufacturers as exporters of these goods. The economy of two cities – Agra for its leather and Ludhiana for knitwear – was then dependent on the Soviet Union.

Within the framework of the five-year Indo-Soviet Trade and Payment Agreement, annual trade talks were held alternately at Moscow and Delhi. Along with the commercial counsellor, H.K. Singh, I was also summoned to Delhi in December 1970 to join the Indian side for trade talks with the visiting Soviet delegation. This time the agenda was to negotiate and work out a five-year trade plan for 1971–75 with the renewal of the existing agreement. The Soviet delegation was led by Mr I. T. Grishin, deputy minister, counterpart of our commerce secretary, Mr K.B. Lal. The working session was conducted by Mr N.P. Jain, joint secretary, and his counterpart, Mr A. Shiriaev, director general, Ministry for Foreign Trade, USSR. The enjoyable part of this annual exercise was the lavish hospitality extended by both sides. Indian public sector bodies organized dinner parties at five-star hotels. Some leading exporters from Ludhiana and Agra used to set up their camps in Delhi to look after and entertain the Soviet delegation members. Sometimes the two sides would meet twice a year, with the Indian delegation visiting Moscow in summer for mid-term review of the annual trade plan. Those were the crowning years of Indo-Soviet friendship.

The Indo-Soviet Joint Commission covering mutual cooperation in diverse economic and industrial sectors also held its annual sessions at Moscow and Delhi. There too I was asked to participate in the foreign trade working group. Further, I was also a regular member of every Indian trade delegation visiting East European countries.

A joyful annual event was the Soviet Film Festival held alternately at Moscow and Tashkent. A delegation of officials from the Indian Ministry of Information and Broadcasting (I&B) and film producers, directors, actors and film journalists were invited to this festival. I was looking after the export of Indian films, then handled by the STC's subsidiary, the Film Export Corporation.

The Soviet festival authorities usually consulted me for finalizing the list of invitees from India. The Soviet organizers extended full hospitality to the guests including air travel. For me, the most memorable was the Tashkent festival in 1972. The Indian delegation led by the I&B minister Nandini Satpathy included Nargis, Sunil Dutt, K.A. Abbas, Sukhdev, F.C. Mehra, and some others. Nargis had a large fan following in Russia since the *Awara* days and she got loud applause when she addressed the audience. It was the first time that Bangladesh, then a newly emerging nation, participated in the Tashkent festival. Pakistan was represented by its famous stars Mohammad Ali and Zeba Ali, the husband-wife duo. Noticing them sitting alone, I invited them to join us at our table where the two Bangladeshi artists were also present. The Russian hosts were both surprised and amused to see us sharing the same table and rushed to click their cameras and present bouquets to the women artistes from three countries.

The Russians used to buy Indian films during this festival. Sunil Dutt, then facing financial difficulties, was anxious to sell his film *Reshma aur Shera*. I had received instructions from the ministry to help him in every possible way. He stayed on in Moscow for a couple of weeks and finally I succeeded in persuading the Russian buyers to take his film. The toughest and most time-consuming job for me was negotiations for the sale of Raj Kapoor's *Mera Naam Joker*, which included the famous Russian Circus performance. Accustomed to paying only two to three lakh rupees for an Indian film, the Russians offered to pay five lakh for it. I pointed out that this amount was not enough even to meet the cost of the Russian Circus's participation. Negotiations dragged on and it was only after intervention by the Soviet Ministry of Foreign Trade that they finally agreed to pay Rs 15 lakh for it. An amusing fallout of my association with the Russian film festival was my encounter with Bollywood stars during my visit to Bombay in December 1972. Sitting in the Harbour Bar of the Taj, I was spotted by the film journalist Mr Parekh who had been to Tashkent. Within a few minutes he brought a couple of well-known actors who promptly invited me for drinks and fancy music parties. They politely hinted at their great interest in visiting Moscow and requested me to recommend their inclusion in the Indian list for the following year's festival. Mr Parekh, however, succeeded in getting my interview and remarks on the prospects of exporting Indian films to Russia and carried it on the front page of *Screen* the next morning.

After the film festival I used to arrange showings at the embassy premises. Video cassettes and DVDs were still unknown and Indian films screened in Moscow were dubbed in Russian, though the songs were retained in the original language. We had a small auditorium which could barely accommodate the embassy staff and their families. I had to put up shows for the Indian community in Moscow including the young students who would pester me for repeat screenings. I recall running *Amar Prem* for one whole week.

We had also some notable performing artists visiting Moscow under the cultural exchange programme. I vividly remember the visit of Begum Akhtar, the ghazal queen, whom I knew very well. Her performance was highly appreciated by the Russian connoisseurs of music. Even without understanding the lyrics they admired her mellifluous voice and the surging strains of the accompanying musical instruments, especially the sarangi. I had attended quite a few private singing sessions of Begum Sahiba at eminent artiste Naina Devi's house in Delhi. She was amazed to hear her own recorded singing which I had preserved for over twenty-five years. Moscow was then a popular destination for Indian VIPs during the summer months. Apart from President Giri and Prime Minister Indira Gandhi, quite a few cabinet ministers also visited Moscow. Then we had official delegations coming all the year round. In the field of commerce, we had regular visits by delegations from different export promotion councils.

Indo-USSR trade was governed by the annual trade plan listing items of import and export with their volume or value. Both sides kept a constant watch on the fulfilment of commitments by either side to ensure the balance. The trade agreement did not envisage any payment in foreign exchange and trade surplus earnings were credited to the non-convertible rupee accounts of either side. The repayment of annual instalments of credits extended by the USSR for export of their defence equipment and other plant and machinery were made through export of Indian goods and services. The rupee trade mechanism embodied in India's trade agreements with the USSR and other socialist countries since the 1960s facilitated a notable expansion of trade with these countries. By 1971 they had emerged as the most important destination for India's exports and surpassed other regions in comparison. During this period the USSR played a dominant role in building up India's heavy industries, especially steel, engineering and power generation in the public sector. The USSR was the first country to offer us the technology and credits for setting up the Bhilai Steel plant in the public sector. Then followed Britain with Durgapur and Germany with Rourkela. As payment was through Indian exports, it gave a great stimulus to Indian industry, especially manufactured products, engineering goods, chemicals and pharmaceuticals, and a wide range of consumer items including handicrafts.

It was a herculean task to introduce new manufactured products in the Russian market. A typical case was of Indian petrol pumps recommended by the Soviet Trade Office in Bombay. Our negotiations with Russian buyers had dragged on until I got a pump air-freighted to Moscow and an Indian engineer was brought to demonstrate its functioning to the satisfaction of the gas station management.

A notable case of a costly extravaganza and also a commercial fiasco was the fanciful project launched by Mrs Pupul Jayakar, head of the Handicrafts and Handloom Exports Corporation of India (HHEC), an STC subsidiary. She was overenthusiastic in promoting export of handloom silk and cotton textiles to the USSR. After surveying the market and discussions with the Soviet trade enterprises as well as the Ministry of Foreign Trade I had informed the STC and the Ministry of Commerce that there was no scope whatsoever for exporting these products. However, Mrs Jayakar was determined and ignored my advice. She wielded considerable influence and power due to her proximity with the prime minister, Mrs Gandhi. So, I was instructed to make all arrangements for a grand fashion show with Russian models. Mrs Jayakar commissioned the leading French designer Pierre Cardin and the famous Japanese designer H. Mori to produce dazzling Western dresses with different varieties of Indian handloom silks. The HHEC was then running a store, Sona, in Paris for the sale of Indian handloom textiles and designed dresses. I had to struggle a lot for organizing this fashion show, the first of its kind to be held by us in Moscow. Fortunately, the head of the India desk in the Ministry of Foreign Trade, G.P. Semenilkov, came to my rescue and helped me in arranging the venue for the show and also in the selection of attractive Russian models who were overzealous to take part in the show. Pierre Cardin also visited Moscow to provide his inputs for the show. Mrs Jayakar deputed Brij Bhushan, the general manager of Sona, to Moscow for assisting me.

The fashion show with its glamour and glitter with beautiful Russian models was hailed as a unique trade promotion exercise. The visiting Russian dignitaries and the diplomatic corps were greatly impressed by the striking range of Indian handloom textiles and fabulous designs of the European dresses. The wonderful show was followed by a grand banquet at Hotel Rossia, where the guest list included everyone from the foreign trade minister to the presidents and senior officials of leading Soviet trading enterprises. Mrs Jayakar was jubilant, hoping that her grand venture was bound to create a new market for her fancy goods. In her encounter with I.T. Grishin, deputy minister of foreign trade, she urged the inclusion of handloom textiles in the trade protocol. Later, during the annual official trade negotiations, the Russian side politely rejected the Indian proposal on the plea that handloom silks and other textiles were far too expensive and not machine washable. Mrs Jayakar did not understand the fact that the state monopoly of foreign trade left no scope for consumer preference and permitted only imports considered essential for the people at large.

The Soviet market was the most sought after by Indian exporters owing to regular bulk orders once the relationship was established with the state enterprises in Moscow. There was a group of influential exporters who always managed to obtain visas for visiting Moscow. Some others lined up to route their exports through the STC on the basis of a fixed commission or service charge. There was also a Russian-sponsored trading company in India, Navbharat, which acted as a middleman on behalf of the Soviet trade enterprises, especially in respect of traditional Indian products like tobacco, coffee, tea and jute. Navbharat earned enormous commissions, part of which were reportedly distributed to the Communist Party of India and also the ruling party. It was quite active for nearly two decades until there were questions about its activities. It came under a cloud during the mid-1970s when it was wound up, but some of its partners managed to set up new firms and carry on their business with Soviet patronage.

Though export of leather footwear and knitwear was routed through the STC, the lists of exporters were established with Russian consent. It was difficult for newcomers to enter this profitable trade. The newcomers tried all means, including political and official influence, in order to get in. I recall some cases of business parties recommended by even cabinet ministers. Another profitable bulk trade was tobacco, monopolized by a select group patronized by the Russian buyers through the USSR trade office in Madras. Most of this trade flourished on personal contacts and mutual trust.

In regard to principal Indian imports from the USSR, the Soviet network was well organized for dealings with the Indian public sector bodies handling these. I would like to mention STC's import of newsprint and the MMTC's of fertilizers. Their delegations with technical and financial experts came to Moscow every year to negotiate the price and delivery terms for the agreed quantities provided in the annual trade plan. The Russian side had their appointed agents who would also come to Moscow to brief them about Indian requirements and other sources of supplies. They would keep in touch with the Indian delegation but were not expected to attend any business meetings. These agents, though earning large commissions, kept a low profile. It was said that they received only a portion of this income. The bulk of it was passed on by them to the political outfits of different hues, select media circles, and the leftist groups as dictated by the Russian principals. There were also instances when trusted Indian exporters were asked to deliver funds to specified destinations.

Both India and the USSR faced shortage of hard currency, and they allocated limited quantities of those goods and raw materials which were free foreign exchange earners. The same restriction applied to manufactured products which had a high import content. The Indian side would press for additional newsprint and fertilizers while Russians demanded more jute, tea, coffee and cashew nuts. In spite of our repeated efforts we could not persuade Russia to include oil in our annual trade plan, but they arranged a triangular deal whereby Iraq supplied oil to India for which we made payment in rupees to the USSR.

Coming to our social life, it was somewhat restricted for diplomats. We could invite only those Russians who had official dealings with us and that too with permission from their offices. A few of them had clearance to socialize with select diplomats. Recalling my past experience in socialist countries, I tried to cultivate some artists who enjoyed relative freedom to meet foreigners. The eminent painter Glazunov and the leading pianist Nelly Akopian were my frequent guests.

Among popular entertainments were the world-famous Bolshoi Ballet Theatre and the Russian Circus. There were favourite restaurants: Aragavi (Georgian), Ararat (Armenian) and the National (Russian). One had to make reservations well in advance to visit them. There were long queues to be seen outside famous eating places including ice cream parlours. It was great fun eating ice cream in biting cold in temperature as low as -20^0 Celsius. There was delightful live music in many restaurants; the most striking I found was at Ararat, the Armenian outlet. It was a wonderful experience to down the famous appetizing Armenian cognac, the favourite of Winston Churchill, with enchanting live music and song. I vividly recall how after a hearty meal and drink I asked my Russian friend to invite the band group for drinks at my place. It was midnight and they were winding up for the day. For them it was a novel experience to visit an Indian home and so they readily agreed to come. This was the most memorable night of my stay in Moscow as I tried to entertain the entertainers with drinks and snacks. They had brought their instruments with them and enchanted us with their soul-stirring airs. Then on their request I played some Indian film music, especially Raj Kapoor's *Awara* songs, their favourite. It was great fun, with everybody in high spirits. After this episode the Ararat management invariably welcomed me even without prior reservation. Another delightful place was the magnificent Arbat Restaurant with a large dancing floor on Leninsky Prospect. Those were the glorious days of Indo-Russian friendship and the pretty Russian dames seldom declined an offer to dance with them. Then there were the foreign currency bars in hotels Metropol and National where we could get imported liquor and wines. These spots had their own special ambience and Russian guests enjoyed being entertained there.

It was a common topic of conversation among diplomats as to who was strictly a professional and who was a KGB official, both working in the same state organization. I usually found the KGB tribe far more interesting and friendly to socialize. Besides, since my field of activity was commerce I had ample opportunity to interact with Russian officials from state trading enterprises. I had a comfortable big office on the ground floor of a big residential bloc at Lomonosovsky Prospect, not far from the Moscow State University. At times I had business meetings there with Russian officials followed by a drink party after office hours. The guards at the diplomatic campus would ask Russian guests coming to visit me to show invitation cards. I was told that the KGB was exempted from this check. In order to overcome this hurdle I gave blank invitation cards to some of my non-official Russian contacts to facilitate their visits to my place. I also visited some Russian homes ranging from a modest one-room apartment far away from the city centre to luxurious ones in the centre where I met some of their best artists from theatre and cinema. I was impressed by the generous and warm hospitality of the Russians. Invariably they would go out of the way to entertain their guests and there was so much human touch in their interaction that they would make anyone feel at home with them.

I enjoyed travelling by bus, train and metro and ambling in the main street near the historic Red Square. In my casual attire I did not attract any attention and was mistaken as someone from the Central Asian republics. I recall an amusing incident near a wine shop when I was approached by a young Russian to go fifty-fifty in buying a vodka bottle and then split its contents, a common practice with workers. I agreed to his proposal and took my share. I found the Russian vodka quite an agreeable drink and most enjoyable when taken along with black rye bread with butter and caviar and chased with mineral water. Also, unlike whiskey, it left no hangover.

The Western tourists in their fancy modern attire walking around in streets caught the attention of the Russian youngsters. I recall once seeing a foreigner stopped by a youngster who offered to buy his leather jacket for a fancy price. There was a craze for all kinds of Western goods including cigarettes and cosmetics. There was a black market for these goods where mostly youngsters were involved including visitors from the other communist countries of East Europe. During the 1960s and '70s, the situation in India was also somewhat similar when all imports of Western consumer goods were practically banned. A lucrative smuggling trade flourished which was even played up by the Western media with photographs of smugglers in action on the western coast of India. All kinds of goods, from synthetic textiles to electronic products, and also liquor and cigarettes, were smuggled in an organized way to feed the black market flourishing in Indian metropolitan cities. The network was so efficient that one could even order for specific items and brands for a price. There was no such organized trade in Moscow and people in general were content with the available goods. It was said that the ruling party elite had an access to some exclusive stores in Kremlin where they could get what they wanted.

In pursuit of their objective to spread communist ideology, the Soviet Union generously offered scholarships to foreign students especially from developing countries to study at their universities.

There were a good number of Indian students in Moscow pursuing their studies in engineering, medicine, humanities and languages. Some of them had lingered on for years to obtain their postgraduate and doctoral degrees. Coming from different parts of India they made a significant contribution in disseminating information about Indian history and culture amongst the student community at large including those hailing from other parts of the world.

Air India flew Delhi–Moscow–Delhi two to three times a week and the crew used to have a stopover for a couple of nights. One Captain Kalia commanded the flights for several years and was a prominent figure in Indian community circles. Then there was a Russian-speaking Air India radio officer, Mr Kushwaha, who maintained his family at Moscow. He was a successful entrepreneur and acted as an agent of some Indian exporters. Those days it was difficult to get fresh vegetables in Moscow. So Air India agreed to carry vegetable baskets free of charge for embassy officials. It was Mr Kushwaha who organized a regular supply chain for individual officers by turns. The officers used to hold dinner parties to coincide with the arrival of their vegetable baskets. We paid only Rs 150 for a 10 kg basket containing seasonal vegetables.

We had an active social life with our colleagues. It was quite a large mission with more than twenty diplomatic officers. Ambassador D.P. Dhar, a politician, did not bother about rank or status and mixed freely with his officers enjoying his drinks and a game of bridge. Among my colleagues, I would like to mention Romesh Bhandari, A.K. Damodaran, H.K. Singh, Surendar Arora, Naresh Kumar and bright young officers Yogesh Tiwari, Sidharth Singh, P.K. Singh and Ronen Sen. Though he was much younger to me I struck a friendship with Ronen Sen who impressed me with his intelligence, sincerity of purpose and of course his straightforward plain speaking.

15

Headquarters: The East Europe Desk

On return to Delhi, I was back to the Ministry of Commerce after a lapse of nearly two decades and took over as deputy secretary (East Europe) in January 1974. I was denied any leave on my transfer from Moscow since the Soviet trade delegation led by their deputy minister I.T. Grishin had arrived for annual trade talks. The Indian side was led by the commerce secretary Y.T. Shah, who was well acquainted with my expertise in the Soviet bloc. This annual event was usually a two-week exercise when there was much feasting in the evenings. In addition to the official reception by the commerce secretary, the STC, MMTC and HHEC also hosted dinner parties for the Soviet delegation. The private sector did not lag behind and offered lavish wining and dining in five-star hotels. The Ludhiana knitwear exporters would set up their camp office in Delhi to look after every member of the visiting delegation.

The Ministry of Commerce was now housed in Udyog Bhawan, quite an unimpressive structure, a far cry from the magnificent North Block which was its abode for decades. The building had shabby dark corridors with rows of rooms on both sides. There was no canteen worth visiting and the stinking toilets were another shocking sight. This brought back memories of my first spell in the ministry when I was delighted by the pleasant ambience of North Block with its spic and span environment. Udyog Bhavan was designed with low roofs suitable for air conditioning which was never installed. With my experience in socialist countries, I was amused to find that cooling during the hot summer months was provided according to the rank of officials with khus tattis, desert coolers and air conditioners. Also, while the officers were accommodated on lower floors, the sections with staff were housed at upper floors, burning hot in summer with squeaking fans only. The North Block on the other hand had outlets in every room for both cooling and heating through a central system installed during the Raj.

There was a good deal of politicking by Indian exporters to raise the quotas since it was profitable to make bulk deals with the single monopoly state enterprise of socialist countries. In some cases, like woollen knitwear and leather footwear, Indian industry was largely dependent on the Soviet market. The bureaucracy played a major role in monitoring the bilateral trade flows with rupee trade countries. There were occasions when a particular country lacked rupee funds in their account which interrupted Indian exports. We would then provide technical credit to that country and facilitate our committed imports from it so as to generate rupee funds for their accounts.

Apart from the reciprocal visits of trade delegations every year, we had also established joint commissions with these countries in order to expand economic and technical cooperation in different fields like mining, oil exploration, shipbuilding, science and technology, machine tools and power generation. The commissions were chaired by a cabinet minister of one of our economic ministries and held annual meetings in partner countries on a reciprocal basis. There were working groups on specific fields of cooperation including one on trade. The Indian side preferred to visit these countries during summer and they in turn chose to come here in the winter months. Sometimes, invitations were extended to individual dignitaries by partner countries to strengthen bilateral economic relations.

I recall the invitation received by K.C. George, then deputy commerce minister in early 1974, from the Hungarian government. I was asked by the commerce secretary to accompany him to Budapest and give him a comprehensive briefing about the rupee payment mechanism and our trade with Hungary. I found K.C. George an extremely pleasant and intelligent person. After a couple of briefing sessions, I asked him if he would like to visit some other neighbouring socialist countries. He said he would love to but there was no invitation. I told him to let me try. I personally knew most of the East European commercial counsellors and through an act of diplomacy, invitations came forth from Czechoslovakia and the German Democratic Republic. I organized a ten-day tour for the deputy minister and also tied up with Air India to have a night stopover at Moscow. The official meetings were fruitful and some pending bilateral issues were settled. Above all, Mr George became a good friend and we kept up contact even after he had left the commerce ministry.

Later in the year, I visited Bulgaria and Romania as a member of the official delegations for annual joint commission meetings. The most memorable trip was to North Korea, when I led a trade delegation to Pyongyang in January 1975. It was an arduous journey via Moscow and that too at the peak of winter season. The Air India flight to Moscow was quite comfortable but after a night halt there we had to take an Aeroflot flight with their propeller aircraft, which took nearly twelve hours with stopovers at Omsk and Irkutsk, the Siberian cities, with temperatures between –40° and –50° Celsius. Finally we landed at Pyongyang the next day, nearly forty-eight hours after our departure from Delhi. Unfortunately, this was the approved route; besides, the only international air links with Pyongyang were via Moscow or Beijing. Anyway, we were given a warm welcome by the North Korean officials with a group of children holding bouquets of flowers. We were now in the land of Kim Il Sung, the supreme beloved leader of the Korean people. I was familiar with the communist countries of Europe, but the Korean brand of communism presented a novel picture in every respect. Our three-member delegation was provided with three official cars and three protocol officials to attend on each one of us. They also occupied adjoining rooms in the hotel where we were lodged. The North Korean trade team was led by their deputy minister. As with the Soviet bloc countries, we had a long-term rupee trade and payment agreement with North Korea as well. The annual trade protocol was concluded with mutual satisfaction.

It was amusing to hear the mention of Kim Il Sung during every discussion. Each official wore a metal badge carrying a picture of the supreme leader. We were not allowed to go out anywhere without an official escort. When we wanted to visit some shopping centre, we were taken to a foreign currency store set up for the diplomats. As we drove on the city streets, there were no crowds or any significant traffic. The most interesting sightseeing tour arranged by our hosts was a visit to the museum dedicated to the life and achievements of the supreme leader in every field of life. There was pictorial narration as to how the supreme leader Kim Il Sung conceived, planned and developed the country's industrial structure and the production of defence equipment from tanks to aircraft, all designed by him. It was indeed a unique experience for me. We felt as if we were in a different world. I learnt more from our ambassador, Ravi Jerath, whose generous hospitality made our stay quite enjoyable.

My return journey from Pyongyang remains an unforgettable experience. I was to return via Tokyo which was only a couple of hours flying time from Pyongyang instead of taking a long haul via Moscow. I took the Korean flight to the Soviet city of Khabarovsk from where I was to catch an Aeroflot flight to the Japanese city of Nigata, which was well connected to Tokyo. When I landed at Khabarovsk I was told that the flight to Nigata was cancelled. Aeroflot flew only twice a week and the next flight was after three days. The Aeroflot manager asked me to buy another ticket to fly to Moscow. I flatly refused to do so and asked him to speak to his seniors and tell them that I had no visa for Khabarovsk. He was quite helpful but said there was a time difference of nearly six hours and people in Moscow were still asleep; so I should wait for another three to four hours. Later, after speaking to the Aeroflot head office at Moscow, he told me that they had instructed him to give me a complimentary air ticket, Khabarovsk–Moscow–Tokyo. So I flew to Moscow by Aeroflot IL-62, an eight-hour flight, landing there late at night. After a few hours stay in the hotel, I was again taken to the airport to catch the Moscow–Tokyo non-stop flight. I landed in Tokyo next day after flying for more than twenty hours instead of two hours as originally scheduled. I had a pleasant three-day stay in Tokyo with my old friend and colleague Y.R. Dhawan, then commercial counsellor in our mission there. It brought back memories of my first diplomatic assignment in Tokyo nearly two decades earlier. I was struck to see Tokyo in its new garb, a magnificent metropolis with elegant tall buildings, modern cars and Japanese men and women in their fashionable attire. One of the familiar spots was the Kabuki Theatre in Ginza, which was as crowded as before. There was no trace of the house I lived in Azabu district. Driving down the main roads of Tokyo,

I was amazed to see the affluence all around demonstrating the economic ascendancy of Japan whose prime minister was once dubbed as a transistor salesman by the French president General de Gaulle. I met our ambassador, S. Than, a kind and unassuming gentleman, and exchanged notes about the current trends in India's trade and economic relations with the Soviet bloc countries. We had known each other for long and the last time we met, he had been our ambassador in Romania.

Back to my desk in Delhi, the Soviet delegation was coming to finalize the next five-year (1976–80) trade agreement for which negotiations had been going on for quite some time. The commerce secretary, S.G. Bose Mullick, was out of station for a bridge tournament and the Russians – mindful about protocol – approached me to do something and ensure that the leader of their delegation, Deputy Minister I.T. Grishin, was received at the airport by a government secretary. I was in a dilemma with this short notice and so I rushed to B.K. Sanyal, secretary (economics) in the Ministry of External Affairs (MEA). I explained our predicament to him and the Russians' concern about protocol. He agreed and received the Russian deputy minister with his delegation. The annual trade plan was finalized and negotiations completed. The Indian delegation was invited to Moscow later in the year to conclude and sign the agreement.

Around early 1975, Commerce Secretary Y.T. Shah, reputed for his honesty and integrity, was unceremoniously transferred to an unimportant post and S.G. Bose Mullick appointed in his place. Later, P.C. Alexander took over from him. Around the same time A.S. Gill, joint secretary (East Europe), was replaced by Prem Kumar. On my part, my transfer to the economic division of the MEA was already pending for some time. With these changes I was asked to stay on and join the delegations led by P.C. Alexander to Prague and later to Moscow. I was known to him from the

1950s during his tenure as deputy secretary in the Ministry of Commerce. He persuaded B.K. Sanyal, economic affairs secretary of the MEA, to let me continue in commerce till the end of 1975. My expertise in East Europe was even more recognized after P.C. Alexander assumed charge. He asked me to act as a tutor to V.P. Singh, then deputy commerce minister (later prime minister), and brief him on the evolution and working of the rupee trade and payment agreements with East European countries. For me, it was quite an amusing experience. He was polite and tried to listen to me over a cup of tea but I found him totally inattentive. During the half-hour I was supposed to spend with him, half the time was lost on his telephone calls from Lucknow. He put no questions nor sought any clarifications. I felt that he was there but his mind was wandering somewhere else. After three or four sessions, he thanked me and said that he would call me when required. I learnt that he wanted to make official visits to some East European countries but then changed his mind.

It was November 1975 when I was again asked by the commerce secretary to join the Indian trade delegation going to GDR since the joint secretary, Prem Kumar, was still new to the job. While in Berlin, I made the task easier for both sides by working out the detailed annual trade plan in a private session with my old friend W. Bruckner, the GDR commercial counsellor in Delhi. At the next day's session, the GDR side informed the Indian delegation that they had accepted our proposals for the trade plan. While I was busy winding up to move over to the MEA, I was asked in December 1975 to accompany the Romanian foreign trade minister to Hyderabad, Bombay and Bangalore. He was here for the Indo-Romanian Joint Commission meeting. It is worth mentioning that though it was India's turn to visit Bucharest for the meeting, the Romanian minister was keen to visit India and so they persuaded us to do this favour. According to corridor gossip, the Romanians had arranged some donations to the ruling party funds. Anyway, the Indo-Romanian Joint Commission concluded their annual session and I bade farewell to the Ministry of Commerce.

For several years I had not availed of any leave, so before joining external affairs, I took a month's leave in January 1976. However, just a week later, I was summoned to duty by the secretary, B.K. Sanyal. He told me to undertake preparatory work and coordinate with other economic ministries to finalize the agenda papers for the forthcoming Indo-Soviet Joint Commission meeting at Moscow in March 1976. The Indian delegation, led by P.N. Haksar, then vice chairman, Planning Commission, included M. Sondhi, secretary, heavy industry; M. Narsimhan, secretary finance; and senior officials from other economic ministries. As member-secretary of the delegation, I was to handle all administrative work and coordinate the activities of different working groups. The ministries would usually put up a long list of officials to join the Indian delegation but it was scaled down by the MEA, since in those days any government delegation going abroad required the formal approval of the prime minister. There was much lobbying and politicking by some officials keen to visit Moscow. I recall how the Ministry of Foreign Trade nominated their economic advisor, Mr Sengupta, with no experience and background, for the working group on trade. In order to avoid any embarrassment, I was asked by the chairman, Mr Haksar, to handle discussions on trade as per the agenda with the Soviet side and finalize the document. Every working group held discussions with its Soviet counterpart reviewing the implementation of earlier decisions during the year and study new proposals from either side to diversify and expand mutual economic cooperation in different fields. The Indian side usually prepared drafts of minutes of the meetings which were finalized after a series of discussions.

It was also an occasion for announcing some new major industrial cooperation projects and some triangular trade deals involving a third country.

The official visits to Moscow were enjoyable with a dose of holiday spirit. The most attractive part were the sightseeing tours of some other Soviet republics, viz., Kazakhstan, Uzbekistan, Georgia, Armenia, Azerbaijan, etc. We were lavishly entertained there with choicest local cuisine, wines and spirits, and some cultural shows. The local officials displayed overflowing warmth and affection with a lot of hugging, marking deep friendship. Incidentally, for the host officials also it was an occasion to entertain themselves.

Soon after our return to Delhi, I got busy with preparations for the Indo-Polish Joint Commission meeting in Warsaw. Our delegation led by Minister K.C. Pant landed there in May 1976. Next to the Soviet Union, Poland was our second largest trading partner in East Europe. I had prepared speeches for the minister and he was quite happy with them. Mr Pant was a gentleman of the core. I gave him company and briefed him about Poland's economy and the social and cultural scene.

Back home, I was still busy clearing the piled up files when I was asked by the foreign secretary Jagat Mehta to join the prime minister's delegation going to Afghanistan and the GDR. The delegation included Syed Mir Kasim, then cabinet minister without portfolio, Principal Secretary P.N. Dhar, Foreign Secretary Jagat Mehta, some other senior officers and a group of media persons.

I vividly remember the historic Kabul meeting of Mrs Gandhi with Afghan president Daud Khan. She was articulate in highlighting the importance of the historic Indo-Afghan political and economic ties with a common cultural heritage. She took pains to explain the domestic circumstances which compelled her to impose Emergency that had received some criticism by the foreign media. At no stage did Mrs Gandhi look at any brief or consulted anyone. I was impressed by her confidence visible during the discussions.

From Kabul we took off for Berlin, the capital of the GDR (German Democratic Republic). During the flight, I observed that practically all officials and media persons named the country of their visit as East Germany and its capital as East Berlin. I knew that our GDR hosts were sensitive in this respect and would take it amiss. I went over to Mir Kasim and suggested that it would be desirable if the PM made an announcement that we were visiting Berlin, the capital of the German Democratic Republic and not East Berlin or East Germany. It worked and Mrs Gandhi came out from her enclosure and announced accordingly.

This was the first visit by an Indian prime minister to the GDR after the establishment of full diplomatic relations with them. It was a special occasion for our GDR hosts to welcome Mrs Gandhi, a leading personality from the Third World. As the high point of bilateral friendly ties was the strengthening and expansion of trade and economic relations, I was asked by Jagat Mehta to join the drafting group for finalizing the joint communique with the GDR to be signed by our prime minister and the GDR president Erich Honecker. I vividly remember that we sat through late in the night with our GDR colleagues to finalize the mutually acceptable draft.

I recall an amusing episode about the return banquet given by our prime minister to the GDR president and his official team. Our embassy had made arrangements but as was customary there was no provision for any alcoholic drinks. Indians were used to this practice and those who enjoyed a drink before dinner would have it before joining the party. I knew it would be hard for our GDR guests to have their dinner without any beer or wine. So I approached Mr Kasim to secure Mrs Gandhi's approval. Then I learnt from him that Mrs Gandhi had merely smiled and retorted that she had never told anyone not to serve beer or wine. Funnily, some senior bureaucrats whispered that Indian members should abstain from taking any drink. It was quite amusing and I told everyone that those who enjoyed a drink should have it with our GDR guests. It was an established practice in Delhi and I think it is still the same that no alcohol is served at functions hosted by ministers. But the secretaries hosting foreign delegations are free to serve all kinds of liquor arranged by our protocol.

Later in 1976, I was appointed as the first consul general at Chicago. With the increased Indian diaspora in the Midwest, there was a great demand for an Indian mission at Chicago. I was told to proceed there in November but was held back to handle the Indo-Romanian Joint Commission meeting at Bucharest in early December 1976. Our delegation was led by Petroleum Minister D.K. Barooah and the official team headed by Secretary B.B. Vohra, my old friend and classmate, for whom it was his first visit to any communist country. The meeting over, we were stranded there as Bucharest airport was closed due to heavy snowfall. The minister had left a day earlier. The Romanian hosts extended their full hospitability and advised us to stay on and await the opening of the airport. As B.B. Vohra was keen to return, I arranged with our embassy to send the two of us by an overnight train to Belgrade, where the Air India office would arrange a suitable return flight via Rome or Frankfurt. So we came to Belgrade and Air India provided us night stopover and booked us on their flight via Rome. For me, it was like a homecoming and I took Mr Vohra around the city, showed him some historic landmarks and wound up the day with dinner at my favourite haunt, the Writers' Club, the famous hub of writers, theatre actors and singers.

My posting to Chicago apparently marked the end of my eventful official link with the socialist world of East Europe. I was satisfied and content with my rich experience and could never then imagine that this was merely the conclusion of Phase I and a far more significant association with these countries awaited me in the near future.

16

Chicago: Farewell to the Foreign Office

I LANDED IN CHICAGO ON 11 February 1977 and was taken straight to my official residence at the Lake Point Tower, then hailed as the tallest residential building in the world. The Indian consulate was opened in December 1976 by a dear colleague and friend, Brij Kumar, who was temporarily appointed as acting consul general after his retirement from New York. He had hired the office at Michigan Avenue, the main street in the city centre. The consulate had started functioning with its staff well established and most of the initial logistic problems had been sorted out thanks to Brij Kumar. But there was no official car and driver for which he had left the choice to me. Interestingly for local staff, our missions in the USA usually hired Indian visitors seeking extension of their visas with an ultimate motive of settling down in the USA. The paltry salary offered by us would not attract any local American.

There was government sanction for the car and driver but I learnt that our embassy at Washington wanted to palm off one of their old cars for the consulate at Chicago and add a new one to their fleet. I took it up with Ambassador Kewal Singh who fortunately expedited the process of procurement of a new car. The next hurdle came up with the government condition that the car should be without an air conditioner and radio, which were standard fittings for American cars. We had to place a special order with General Motors, Detroit, to supply us this bare model. It took nearly two months before a Chevrolet Impala of this type was delivered to us. Then one Indian, a qualified engineer in need of a visa extension, was hired as a driver. I mention it because later the US State Department issued orders stopping this practice by foreign missions in the USA.

Chicago, the second largest city in the US, was one of the leading centres of trade and industry in the world. Also a seat of learning and higher education, the city took pride in Chicago University with its reputed department of South Asian studies. It had renowned scholars like Professors Lloyd and Susanne Rudolf, Edward C. Demock Jr, and Milton Singer who had made notable contributions to the scholarly achievements of the American Institute of Indian Studies. I opened my innings in Chicago by calling on these eminent persons and nursed my association with Professors Lloyd and Susanne Rudolf.

The Indian presence in Chicago was already established with the offices of Air India, State Bank of India, Engineering Export Promotion Council and India Tourist Centre. By 1977 there was a sizable Indian population, including a large number of students pursuing studies in different fields. By and large Indians occupied good positions both in academia as well as the corporate world. There were a good number of medical doctors, specialists and surgeons holding responsible posts in leading hospitals. A few of them even ran medical centres with government funding under national security for the poor African Americans in south Chicago. There was also a trading community who had turned Devon Street of Chicago into a regular Indian bazaar with a variety of shops and restaurants. A number of them had come as students with the intention of earning a bit and returning home, but most of them never went back and chose to settle down here. They went home only to pick up Indian brides and bring them to America. Those were the days when the green card holders enjoyed a preference in the Indian marriage bazaar.

The Indian diaspora in Chicago was dominated by the Gujarati community. Among the leading figures of the community, I found Naren Somi a pleasant gentleman ever willing to help others. He owned Patsons Travel, a leading travel agency with branches in New York and Los Angeles. He owned the leading Indian restaurant Khyber and also ran a medical centre with Thakar Patel as his partner. India League of America, probably the oldest Indian association in the USA, had its Chicago chapter led by Manoj Singhvi, a prominent engineer with a US multinational. There were quite a few others who organized community functions and maintained close contact with the Indian consulate. The Indian community in the USA comprised first-generation immigrants, most of whom had come during the 1960s and '70s. They had their roots in India and usually made annual trips home to meet their families. They were naturally keen to keep abreast with the happenings at home. A weekly *India Abroad* published from New York was a popular source of Indian news. Two enterprising Indian ladies from Chicago – Rama Deva and Vichitra Nayyar – had brought out a bimonthly, the *Indic Magazine*, which carried not only news from the subcontinent but also about the events and functions organized by different sections of the Indian community all over America. Another publication that came out after my arrival was the *India Tribune*, a weekly edited by Thakar Patel.

The Indian community in Chicago had grown in recent years and was now the second largest after New York. There were frequent community functions, celebration of festivals and concerts of visiting Indian performing artists. Vichitra Nayyar set up a community radio service followed by her TV show *Chitrahar*. She promoted talented local singers and musicians and also assisted me in organizing monthly musical evenings at my house. I still remember the harmonium and tabla duo Mohammad Ali and Williams, and singers like Sheetal Chowdhry and Mohammad Shujat. A great activist and community leader, Vichitra had interviewed three Indian prime ministers on their visits to Washington. She and her engineer husband Sarv Nayyar became my lifelong friends.

Chicago was a popular destination for every leading singer coming from the subcontinent and I was invariably invited as a chief guest. We had Lata Mangeshkar, Asha Bhosle, Mukesh, Kishore Kumar, Runa Laila and Noor Jehan. I recall an interesting episode about Noor Jehan's concert where I was invited as the chief guest since Pakistan did not have their mission in Chicago. I told the organizers that I was her ardent fan and would love to come but they should obtain Noor Jehan's approval. So when the organizers approached her for it, she asked if I was 'dark and ugly'. She gladly agreed when told that I was a Lahoria and her fan.

I am reminded of Indian participation in the Chicago Film Festival in 1978. Satyajit Ray came with his film *Shatranj ke Khiladi* and Shyam Benegal sent his film *Nishant*. I had organized a big reception for Ray and his team. He was overconfident that his film would win the award but it was *Nishant* which was selected. Incidentally, I went out of the way to welcome Ray but was disappointed by his arrogance and aloofness, which was however compensated by his leading actor Saeed Jaffrey, a renowned artist and a perfect gentleman.

Soon after my arrival I had the first house guest, my old time mentor Prakash Tandon, who was on a lecture tour at the invitation of Chicago University. I was all by myself without my family and domestic help. However, he felt quite at home and even taught me some cooking. He told me about the old maxim: 'If you wish a thing to be well done, you must do it yourself.' After watching him wash his shirts and polish his shoes, I learnt the art of independent living, which proved useful a few years later when I was with the United Nations in Geneva.

The first prominent Indian to call on me was Swami Rama, famous for his Himalayan Institute of Yoga and Philosophy set up in Chicago with the support of his American disciples. He had links with some leading Indian politicians and later figured prominently in the Indian political scene. Soon after my coming to Chicago, Prime Minister Indira Gandhi had announced general elections in March 1977. The Congress lost and the Janata Party led by Morarji Desai assumed office on 24 March 1977. The Janata Party was not formed on the basis on any common ideology or an economic programme. It was a heterogeneous group which set no targets except a post-mortem of the excesses of the Emergency and desperately sought to humiliate Mrs Gandhi.

The new government appointed the eminent jurist Nani Palkhiwala as our ambassador in Washington DC, replacing Kewal Singh, who was a popular figure among Indians. Though a large section of Indians were critical of Mrs Gandhi's excesses during the Emergency, she had regained their respect after her gracefully relinquishing power and upholding the sanctity of democracy. Ambassador Palkhiwala – in his lectures to the Indian community groups and also during his meetings with the academia at Chicago and other universities – harped on his criticism of Mrs Gandhi and her government. He behaved like a jurist and was thus not suited for the ambassador's post. To add to that, the new Janata government's entire attention towards persecution of Mrs Gandhi and her supporters, and the launching of enquiries into the excesses of the Emergency soon disillusioned the Indian diaspora. Janata party leaders had nothing in common with each other except their hatred for Mrs Gandhi. Their famous Shah Commission's actions were ridiculed as they rebounded to the favour of those accused rather than against them.

The *Chicago Tribune*, after their long interview with me, came out with an editorial praising Mrs Gandhi for relinquishing power and submitting to the mandate of the people. The new government's efforts to arrest and punish Mrs Gandhi proved to be counterproductive and the same Indian diaspora who had criticized Mrs Gandhi just a year earlier now ridiculed the antics of the new leaders. I tried my best to enlighten Ambassador Palkhiwala about the current situation and even advised him to speak about the new government's policies and achievements instead of about Mrs Gandhi. However, it had no effect and he continued with his tirade against Mrs Gandhi. Incidentally, it was the same Palkhiwala who was engaged by Mrs Gandhi in 1975 to file an appeal in the Supreme Court against the Allahabad High Court order against her. Having agreed to appear, he later refused to fulfil his professional commitment which was totally against the professional code of conduct. The saving grace was that Foreign Minister Atal Bihari Vajpayee, who commanded respect, continued with the existing foreign policy of non-alignment and invoked the names of Gandhiji and Pandit Nehru in his speeches and lectures. It is a pity that he could not visit Chicago during his official visits to New York.

In 1978, Swami Rama organized a conference in Chicago to promote his yoga institution and enlarge his following. He was a colourful personality and I was impressed by his oratory and knowledge. A handsome man, immaculately dressed whether in Western attire or in holy robes, he had perfected the art of mesmerizing people. He had welcomed me in his institution with a lavish lunch attended by over a hundred of his American followers.

He had more than ample funds and it was even rumoured that he had CIA connections. Incidentally, he told me that he had paid the entire medical expenses of Jayaprakash Narayan in the US. He even hinted that I could approach him for funds to help out any Indian in distress. Despite his proximity to JP, he claimed to have intimate contacts with Congress leaders as well. Around this time another godman, Chandraswamy, appeared on the scene. He was supposedly sent by some influential quarters in Delhi to join Swami Rama. However, Swami Rama told me that he had nothing to do with him and could not take him in his institution. Chandraswamy was not disheartened and as I knew about his political contacts in Delhi, I arranged his spiritual lecture session at the consulate where prominent local Indians were invited. I collected voluntary donations and gave these to Chandraswamy. He was, however, far more practical and clever and soon enlisted a few disciples from among the business community who took charge of him and even helped him pick up some disciples in New York. It was reported that he had attained siddhi and was capable of performing miracles which helped him enlist some American followers as well. No wonder, he even turned a politician godman in later years.

Returning to some interesting episodes during my tenure at Chicago, I would like to cover the field of Indo-US trade. The Engineering Export Promotion Council had its representative office at Chicago headed by Mr Bakshi. Interestingly, his two predecessors had resigned after completing their term and settled down in Chicago running their own business. It was pointless to have this representation here when it contributed little to promote exports of Indian engineering products.

Mohan Dharia, commerce minister of the Janata government, accompanied by the secretary, P.C. Alexander, held a conference of all heads of missions in the two Americas. It was to review our foreign trade with these countries and explore new ways and means to expand and diversify our trade flows with this region. The minister spoke on the government policy and the need to project India as an emerging industrialized country with a competitive edge in supplying industrial products and manufactured goods. Most participants sought expansion of their commercial sections and recommended participation in their respective country's trade fairs, organize buyer–seller meets and hold exclusive Indian exhibitions. They received support from the representatives of the Trade Fair Authority. On my part I stated that it was pointless to hold Indian exhibitions or participate in the local fairs without ascertaining the export potential of Indian products. I pointed out that the new trend was the holding of specialized trade shows covering a specific industrial sector, citing the case of the Hardware Show in Chicago where there was no government participation, but a couple of enterprising Indian exporters had succeeded in procuring export orders. On the other hand, the great buyer–seller meet organized by the Indian government at Chicago, with the assistance of ITC (International Trade Centre), Geneva, was a flop. It was only a meeting venue for the home Indians with overseas Indians. No one liked my statement but fortunately Mr Alexander, who knew me well, told the audience that I happened to be a trade expert and my views deserved due consideration.

In April 1978, we had another interesting event, organized by the Ministry of Commerce in collaboration with ITC Geneva, at Costa Rica where India's trade representatives stationed in the two Americas were invited to participate. The objective was to finalize the Manual of Instructions for Indian commercial officers posted abroad. It was an enjoyable five-day holiday for everyone. The ITC experts gave lectures and sought suggestions and recommendations from the participants. I surprised everyone when I told them that I was associated with the compiling of the first edition of this Manual under the guidance of K.B. Lal, joint secretary in the Ministry of Commerce during the 1950s. Anyway, the ITC expert, Claude Cellich, who was conducting the group discussion was much impressed with my extensive experience as a commercial diplomat and my expertise in trading with the Soviet bloc countries. He asked me to fill up the UN application form for the position of a consultant. It was a cumbersome task but he insisted and helped me out. Soon after that he was posted as the ITC representative in India. The Ministry of Commerce had decided to bring out a 'Manual on Trading with the USSR and GDR' to serve as a guide for Indian businessmen. They sought the ITC's financial assistance for this project which involved a field study in these countries by a research fellow of the Indian Institute of Foreign Trade. The ITC was requested to provide a consultant to supervise this study. The ITC agreed to fund the project but regarding the consultant, Claude Cellich told the Ministry of Commerce that the ITC knew only one expert in the field who could act as a consultant and that was the Indian consul general at Chicago. He added that the ITC would meet all expenses of his travel, etc., as well as his entitled consultation fee. The Ministry of Commerce prevailed upon the MEA to let me act as a consultant to ITC for their project. It was in October 1978 that I travelled to Geneva where the Indian research fellow Mr Ghosh joined me. We travelled to Moscow where I arranged meetings with the concerned authorities and institutes and collected all relevant information and data. Thereafter, we repeated the exercise in Berlin. My old personal contacts in both countries facilitated the task.

At Moscow, the ambassador I.K. Gujral invited me to stay with him. Incidentally, both I.K Gujral and his wife Sheela Gujral née Bhasin were my classmates in the University of Punjab, Lahore, and we took our MA (economics) degrees together in 1943. The week I spent with them remains etched in my memory. I had met

Mr Gujral when he was information minister, earlier in Moscow and we had renewed our association of student days. I acquainted him with my Russian contacts who had helped me in collecting information for the planned Manual on Trading with the USSR. During my stay, the most enjoyable part was the celebration of Diwali, with just the three of us in the illuminated environment of our embassy residence.

Some colleagues in the Ministry of External Affairs were rather jealous of me and imagined that I had somehow manipulated this consultancy with the ITC: So the ITC was told not to pay me any consultation fee which then amounted to about six thousand dollars. For me it was a rewarding assignment as I was able to establish contacts with the ITC at Geneva which was then headed by P.C. Alexander, former commerce secretary, who knew me well and also my expertise on the Soviet bloc. He introduced me to the Division of Trade with Socialist Countries of the UNCTAD, then headed by a Russian, Mr Davidov. Another lucky coincidence was my meeting with an old friend from the Ministry of Commerce, S. Ramachandran, who was simply thrilled to see me and remarked that providence had sent me to him. He was the principal consultant with UNCTAD for preparing the UNDP project for the development of trade and economic relations between the socialist and the developing countries. He told me that he had just finalized the project and was thinking about a suitable person he could recommend for implementing the project. He had declined UNCTAD's offer to do it owing to his advanced years and inability to undertake the extensive travel involved. He introduced me to UNCTAD officials and recommended me for the post of project director. There were, of course, other candidates, including one proposed by the Government of India, but my fifteen years of experience handling India's trade and economic relations with Soviet bloc countries was unrivalled. I was given an assurance by my long-standing Russian contacts that I would be offered this appointment after the completion of formalities in two to three months.

Back in Chicago, my family had gone on home leave and I too requested for a month's leave to which I was entitled. Strangely, I was denied home leave and given transfer orders to Delhi. I learnt later that some ministry officers were, instrumental in my premature transfer from Chicago, an outcome of the jealousy mentioned. Fortunately, my transfer proved to be a blessing in disguise since at the same time I received an offer from UNCTAD for the post of programme coordinator for the UNDP project mentioned above. I readily accepted the offer and requested for a three-month period to join the post in Geneva. Immediately on my return to Delhi, I sought premature retirement in May 1979 and bade final goodbye to the Government of India after serving it for thirty-five years. Once again, the Ministry of External Affairs, while trying to punish me with an early transfer from Chicago, unknowingly benefited me. Strange are the dictates of destiny.

17

Rewarding Years with the UNCTAD

THE UNCTAD FROM ITS INCEPTION IN 1964 played a pioneering role in promoting trade and economic relations among countries having different economic and social systems, in particular between developing countries and socialist countries of East Europe termed as East–South. The UNCTAD division of trade with socialist countries undertook studies for the purpose. In the light of deliberations at various UNCTAD sessions, it was recognized that one of the main deterrents to increased trade flows between developing countries and socialist countries of East Europe was the lack of information and knowledge about foreign trade systems and trading modalities of these countries. In most of the developing countries, there was also a lack of trained personnel who could identify and explore trading opportunities with socialist countries.

Recognizing the growth prospects in this field, the first phase of the UNDP/UNCTAD technical assistance programme was implemented in 1975–76. The experience confirmed that training and dissemination of information were important elements in facilitating trade expansion and economic cooperation between the two groups of countries. In the light of the foregoing, the second phase of the UNDP/UNCTAD Comprehensive Programme of Technical Assistance (1979–82) was formulated after consultations with UNDP, the UN Regional Commissions and the International Trade Centre, as well as a number of developing countries and socialist countries.

I joined duties in UNCTAD, Geneva, as programme coordinator of this project in September 1979. The comprehensive programme had three main elements: group training, advisory services and dissemination of information. My extensive experience of dealing with socialist countries helped me a great deal in planning and organizing training workshops and seminars for representatives from the developing countries. Over the years, India had emerged as the socialist countries' leading trade partner and with its considerable experience it served as a useful example for other developing countries. Well acquainted with foreign trade regimes, trading practices and the payment arrangements of these countries, I felt confident of advising them in this regard.

My project implementation team included a Czechoslovak consultant, Mr Kubanak, and S. Gueria, an Algerian. Before formulating the work programme it was necessary to negotiate with the socialist countries about the specific workshops/seminars they would agree to host, and then finalize the timing and other logistics. So, along with the UNCTAD finance director we visited Moscow, Warsaw, Berlin and Prague and discussed our planned programme of activities with the authorities concerned and worked out the schedule. The objective was to utilize the UN funds of their non-convertible currencies. For the travel of participants, it was decided to use Aeroflot and other East European airlines wherever they were operating. Fortunately, I knew most of the officials we met in these countries, which greatly facilitated our negotiations.

My next task was to finalize the regional components of the comprehensive programme in consultation with UN Regional Commissions. Along with Mr Gueria, I visited the Economic Commission for Africa at Addis Ababa. After lengthy discussions for three days we finalized the regional project document. Then followed my visit to Bangkok for consultations with the Economic and Social Commission for Asia and the Pacific (ESCAP). Their foreign trade division had already prepared a tentative plan of the seminar-cum-study tour for participants from the Asia-Pacific region. The plan was discussed and an agreed programme was finalized. As considerable amount of preparatory work was involved for the international workshops/seminars I left it to Mr Gueria to visit the UN Economic Commission for Latin America at Mexico and finalize the programme for the regional workshop-cum-study tour.

Inter-regional workshops on trade promotion, trade policy and for trade representatives required considerable planning and preparations in consultation with the host countries Bulgaria, GDR and the USSR. So I visited these countries and finalized the work programme and contents of the workshops.

The comprehensive programme was completed in December 1982. I acted as chairman at all workshops/seminars where experts from socialist countries also joined to deliver lectures followed by discussions.

For dissemination of information, we had to bring out a 'Manual on Trading with Socialist Countries of Eastern Europe'. The International Institute for Economic Problems of World Socialist System, Moscow, was commissioned to prepare the draft. After going through it. I found it too theoretical and full of communist ideology. So I entrusted the task to the Indian Institute of Foreign Trade with a payment of one lakh rupees as fees. They in turn sent a compilation of cyclostyled literature published as guides for Indian exporters to socialist countries including irrelevant information about Indian embassies, commercial sections, etc. I discreetly set it aside and informed the director, Mr Davidov, that I did not approve either of those drafts and took the responsibility to do it myself. It could not be brought out by December 1982 but was published in March 1983. It contained practical information on socialist countries, institutions, trade agreements, payment arrangements, economic cooperation agreements and trading practices.

As regards advisory services, in response to requests received by UNCTAD, I went to Nigeria, Algeria, Peru, Nicaragua and India and advised their governments on specific matters relating to their trade and economic relations with the socialist countries of East Europe. I also organized national seminars there to educate each country's officials and businessmen about the trading opportunities in socialist countries.

The evaluation of the programme was undertaken by an external UNDP team led by the eminent UNCTAD expert R.D. Pradhan, an old friend and colleague of mine from the Ministry of Commerce. The team in its report acknowledged that the programme had played a useful role in promoting trade and economic relations between the two groups of countries. Recognizing the need for technical assistance activities to be continued in this field, the team also recommended a new follow-up programme. The UNDP in its comments on the report recognized that the comprehensive programme had performed a real service as a multilateral instrument in promoting East–South trade but expressed its inability to continue financing these activities beyond December 1982. It suggested that these activities should become a normal function of the UNCTAD Division of Trade with socialist countries.

UNCTAD now launched its Operational Programme of Technical Assistance with the same aims and objectives. I was asked to continue to head the programme as UNCTAD principal adviser/consultant. The new programme was financed by UNCTAD's own limited resources, supplemented by the allotment from trust funds, as well as by voluntary contribution from the socialist countries of East Europe.

I reshaped the programme activities in the light of reduced funds. The inter-regional workshops were now designed to answer the needs of the trade representatives/economic counsellors of developing countries stationed in the socialist counties. The principal aim was to assist them in performing their functions and to enlighten them about the new trends and developments in socialist countries' economies. I organized six such workshops during 1983–85, three in Moscow and one each in Warsaw, Prague and Berlin. In India, I organized a national seminar in Delhi in 1982 in collaboration with the Indian Institute of Foreign Trade.

This six-year (1979–85) tenure with UNCTAD formed the most rewarding years of my working life. I was able to travel extensively and visit the developing world in three continents. This gave me an opportunity to interact with people of different races and cultures and learn about their lifestyles, attitudes, outlook and manners. It was a lively experience to spend two to three weeks together with the same group and socialize with them in the evenings. The most memorable was the Latin American group which I found lively and fun-loving. After spending a week in Moscow we had study tours of Budapest and Prague before concluding the workshop in Havana. Once we had a weekend party which continued till past midnight in the hotel restaurant. In the morning when I came there for breakfast I saw four of them already in the restaurant. When I asked how they had come so early, they replied to my great amusement that they had never left the place and were enjoying their morning dose of wine. I remember this event all the more since in Havana the bus carrying us went off the road and overturned, the driver having gone to sleep. A few of us including myself were injured. The Cuban hosts including their minister suggested my staying on for treatment but I managed to escape and fly to Chicago where I had access to better care, thanks to my friends in the medical field. I informed the UNCTAD administration in Geneva who agreed to my staying on in Chicago for medical treatment. After a week or so, I was able to fly back to Geneva.

It was in December 1985 that I wound up everything in Geneva and returned to India. The best part of this UN tenure was the financial aspect. For the first time in my working life I was able to save sufficient funds for my comfortable post-retirement years. Also, my expertise was duly recognized and acclaimed in UNCTAD circles. In the following years, I was invited once or twice a year for short-term consultancy. So much so, I was unanimously elected as chairman of the experts group meeting organized by UNCTAD in 1987. Then in 1990, I was engaged for a month in Turkey for preparing a UNDP project for development of Turkey's trade and economic relations with the Central Asian republics.

Soviet President Gorbachev's glasnost (openness) and perestroika (reorganization) brought about radical changes in his country's economic and foreign trade system and management. After the fall of the Berlin Wall, East European countries were making their exit from communism. Finally, with the disintegration of the Soviet Union in 1991, the communist system came to an end and as a consequence my long-standing expertise became irrelevant.

Coming to the life in Geneva, my six-year stay there was a delightful experience, more so for my family and grandchildren who spent summer months in the salubrious environment of

Geneva. Though a small town it had the ambience and attraction of a metropolitan city. With the presence of UN offices and several other international organizations like International Labour Organization (ILO), World Health Organization (WHO), and International Telecommunication Union (ITU), Geneva presented a multicultural scene. There was a small affluent Indian community mostly working in these organizations, who got together to celebrate Indian festivals and shared an active social life. My old colleague and friend Raj Bhandari was the virtual community leader who went out of the way to help everyone, especially the new arrivals in Geneva.

I recall an amusing incident of my acting as a marriage priest. One of my friends and neighbours, A.L. Kumar, had made all arrangements to celebrate his daughter's marriage. The bridegroom had also landed in Geneva with a small family group. But there was no trace of the Brahmin priest from London who had been engaged for the ceremony. Raj Bhandari knew that I was a Brahmin with a working knowledge of Sanskrit. He brought Kumar and requested me to rescue him from this dilemma. Kumar gave me an Arya Samaj booklet containing Sanskrit couplets prescribed for the marriage ceremony and also the sequence of rituals to be followed. I agreed to do the needful. Keeping awake till late hours, I studied the scriptures with their Hindi translation so as to fulfil my task as a professional and not to falter at any step. The next day, I presented myself in a white kurta pyjama with a Gandhi cap and long scarf on my shoulder. The venue had a regular stage where I sat on the floor, lighted the fire and directed the bride and groom to occupy their seats and listen to my instructions. The show was watched by a multiracial crowd of guests.

I performed the ceremony with confidence, chanting Sanskrit shlokas with practised diction. Thereafter, I made the couple circle the fire with the accompaniment of my louder recitation. Finally I made them sit, declaring them man and wife. The audience stood up clapping loudly, shouting congratulations and blessings to the newlyweds. To my delight, I was also showered with flowers. It was indeed an exhilarating experience for me.

Another delightful experience etched in my memory is the qawali evening at my house. My long-standing friend Naina Devi, a renowned artist, had come to Geneva with the famous Jaffar Hussain qawali team under the cultural exchange programme. I invited her along with the group for dinner at my place. Knowing my fondness for music, she persuaded Jaffar Hussain and his team to carry their musical instruments with them. I requested them for a performance. Despite it being an audience of one, my enthusiasm was rewarded in the form of a beautiful performance. This reminded me of a scene in the 1950s film *Azad* where the hero Dilip Kumar, all by himself, is listening to a qawali performance with a hit melody '*Marna bhi mohabbat mein kisi kam na aaya*' (Even sacrifice of life served no purpose in love).

18

Turning Writer and Author

MY FIRST FORAY INTO FREELANCE WRITING was way back in 1949 when I earned twenty-five rupees for my article 'Problem of the Mother-in-law' published in *Caravan* magazine. Once, free from working life, I made up my mind to turn a writer. Back in Delhi in 1987, I was well settled at my ancestral house in East Patel Nagar. Now began my daily visits to India International Centre, treating it like my office, spending most of my time in the library. To begin with I tried to use my professional expertise to write on economic subjects. My maiden piece on the flight of capital and criticism of engaging a foreign agency, Fairfax, to discover Swiss accounts of Indians, was considered too controversial to be published. So, I got it published in *India Abroad* in New York. Thereafter, this piece was carried by *Hindustan Times* and some others. I wrote a few more articles dealing with India's trade and economic relations with East Europe and the future of the rupee trade.

Since the communist system had come to an end, I diverted my attention to social and cultural subjects including performing arts and their practitioners. I had a long-standing yearning for writing about my hometown Lahore of the bygone era. I was equally keen to study the life and times of Indian nautch girls – tawaifs or courtesans – accomplished in dance and music who had been banished from the entertainment scene. The pursuit of this study stimulated my interest in the study of women, romance and sex subjects which had a much wider readership.

During my frequent visits to Moscow, I had witnessed the blossoming of Russians in the glow of Gorbachev's glasnost and perestroika. The year 1988 witnessed the first ever beauty contest held in Moscow with 2,500 contestants. The feminine role of women as wives or mothers was receiving far greater attention than as operators of machines. They even held a ticketed show 'Sex and Us' for women only to a packed house. The sexual revolution of the 1970s in the West had proclaimed sexual freedom and permissiveness and also a liberal attitude to pre-marital and extramarital sex. Soviet society could not remain immune to these developments, and with glasnost new attitudes towards sex were finding expression. In order to gauge my readership I wrote an article 'Sex and Glasnost'. I was thrilled to find it published promptly by *Hindustan Times* (7 June 1989) on its op-ed page. Though a few of my articles had earlier appeared in the press, this was the first time that some of my friends called me up to congratulate me for such an entertaining piece. I was overjoyed and considered it as a signal affirming the birth of a writer in me.

Brimming with confidence, I eagerly pursued my research and study for *Nautch Girls of India* in the British library during my annual visits to London. I also explored the sketches and paintings of nautch girls by British and Indian artists held by the museums and galleries there. After I had acquired my first set of about twenty images in the form of 35 mm slides, I worked for over a month to produce my illustrated piece 'The Nautch Girl and the Sahib'. This was published as a cover story in the new year (1990) issue of the *India Magazine*, then the leading publication on Indian people and culture. It was spread over ten pages of the magazine with rare pictures appearing in print for the first time. Incidentally, I was the first writer to cover the subject.

As I had made an extensive study of the sahibs' social and cultural life in India, I wrote a piece, 'Raj Escapades', which was promptly published by *Debonair* (June 1990), then the only Indian adult magazine. Interestingly, in the next few months they carried three more articles of mine: 'Fazal: Ace Pimp of Lahore', 'Geisha Evenings' and 'A Dance of Fireflies' ('Zinda Nautch Te Gana').

In the meantime I met Khushwant Singh, courtesy our Professor Prem Kripal, his close friend. I requested him to glance through some of my writings carried by *Debonair* and was encouraged on learning that he had enjoyed reading my piece 'Sex and Glasnost' in *Hindustan Times*. I told him about my two planned books on Lahore and nautch girls. After looking at the titles of my *Debonair* articles, he laughed and suggested I should carry on with ticklish subjects like 'Fazal: Ace Pimp of Lahore' and give priority to my Lahore book. So I began working earnestly to complete it. In the process, I realized that newspaper articles had temporary life whereas a book makes one an author. I was reminded of an old saying: If you want your son to remember you, build a mud house, your grandson to remember you, build a pucca house and if your great-grandson to remember you, write a book.

I wanted to cover the social and cultural scene of Lahore of my days. Instead of telling the story of my life, which was anything but extraordinary, I wished to reinvent the atmosphere that existed in the first half of the twentieth century in that great, much loved city of Lahore: a lifestyle, a certain mode of thought and living, now dead and gone. A city is not merely its bazaars and buildings. It is its ambience, moods of joy and sorrow, madness and sadness, fun and excitement and, above all, its people who constitute its soul. I wanted to recapture all these aspects of the city. My desire was to take the reader on a pilgrimage to my Lahore of a bygone era of peace and plenty. I met Lahorias on both sides of the border all over the world where I travelled. I would like to mention one of the most unforgettable incidents which spurred my resolve to write the book on Lahore. In November 1963, I was having breakfast in Hotel Astoria in Geneva when I heard someone calling me in Punjabi, perhaps guessing from my looks, '*Motian waleo, Hindustan de ho ke Pakistan de?*' (Prince of Pearls, are you from India or Pakistan?). I responded promptly, '*Bashao aao baitho, main Lahore da hain*' (Your Royal Highness, please come and sit down, I hail from Lahore). He happened to be a Pakistani from Lahore. It took just a few minutes before we became friendly like ghee and khichdi and were talking about our glorious city I had left sixteen years back. The conversation released a flood of memories deeply impressed on my mind for all these years. I made it my mission to commit them to paper.

As I wanted to give a contemporary flavour to my book, I looked through the microfilms of leading Lahore newspapers, *Tribune* and *Civil and Military Gazette*, covering the period 1920 to 1947. I picked up popular advertisements of the time ranging from cosmetics, tonics, cigarettes, wines, cycles, cars and even sex manuals for husbands and wives, and went on to include advertisements of exhibitions, amusement parks and of course cinema. For contemporary photographs and historic sketches of the Lahore scene, I went to the British Library, London.

This being my first full-length literary work, it was not easy to get any of the leading publishers to take it up. I was still exploring when I met my old Lahore friend Balraj Bowry, an eminent figure from the Indian Information Service, who had worked as press adviser with Prime Minister Indira Gandhi. After retirement he was then working as adviser with the well-known Allied Publishers. Thanks to him, they agreed to publish my book in hard cover within a year. I was thrilled to receive an advance copy of *Lahore: A Sentimental Journey*, donning an author's cap on 22 October 1992, my seventieth birthday. The first book review was by Khushwant Singh. He hailed it as an extraordinary book to be enjoyed by old Lahorias. There was a series of reviews carried by practically all leading newspapers and journals, acclaiming it as the most comprehensive and colourful portrayal of the famous city of Lahore. A few of them carried long excerpts from it. Among the most noteworthy reviews were those by eminent Punjabis, Professor V.N. Datta, Prakash Tandon, the management guru, John Lall, ICS and B.B. Vohra. Further, Prof. Ian Talbot of Coventry University, an authority on Punjab, wrote: 'A lovingly produced portrayal of the city Lahore of the late colonial era is brought alive in a manner in which it has never been before. The book deserves a wide readership'.

Noting its market potential in Pakistan, an enterprising firm, Indus Publications, Karachi, tied up with Allied Publishers and got copies printed by them with their logo. My book received a good amount of publicity in Pakistan and turned a useful source of information about the social and cultural milieu of the city before Partition. One publisher even brought out an Urdu edition *Lahore Jab Jawan Tha* (When Lahore Was Young).

A revised edition of the book, incorporating some additional chapters and more information as suggested by some readers, was brought out by HarperCollins Publishers India in 1997 to coincide with the golden jubilee of Indian Independence. Again, it was widely acclaimed by the media with a plethora of reviews including quite a few in Pakistani newspapers as well. Khalid Hasan, one of the leading Pakistani journalists wrote: 'It is ironic that memories of Lahore have been written and published in India rather than in Pakistan'. Another eminent literary figure of Lahore, Shoaib Hashmi, remarked that he got his money's worth many times over without reading the book but just by viewing the old photographs and facsimiles of newspaper advertisements. The third edition of the book was brought out by Penguin Books in 2006. This time, a launch was held at the India Habitat Centre and the book was released by the Pakistan high commissioner, Shahid Malik.

Soon after the appearance of the Penguin edition at the Delhi Book Fair in 2007, Ms Ameena Saiyid of Oxford University Press, Karachi, tied up with Penguin Books to publish a Pakistani edition. The book was launched at a colourful function organized at my alma mater, Government College, Lahore, in October 2007. It was extensively covered by the media, and Khalid Hasan proclaimed me as 'chalta phirta Lahore' like Saadat Hasan Manto was 'chalta phirta Bombay'.

It was my book on Lahore that got me an invitation from the University of Texas at Austin to deliver a lecture on 'Lahore 1947' at a South Asia seminar held in September 1997. Again, I was invited by Coventry University in England to make a special presentation on the city of 'Lahore: The Paris of the East' at the conference on Punjab organized by them in 2001, and attended by scholars from both Punjabs – Indian and Pakistani – as well as the Punjabi diaspora. Bapsi Sidhwa, a renowned writer from Pakistan, considered me her favourite author by including two chapters from my book in her work *City of Sin and Splendour: Writings on Lahore*. She even asked me to join her in readings when her book was launched by Penguin Books in Delhi in 2005.

I was now considered a specialist on Lahore. A fascinating episode worth mentioning is my involvement in a young English lady Penny Thomson's research relating to her Indian grandfather,

Inder Singh of Lahore. She visited India in 1996 and got interested in genetic inheritance. Then she approached Prof. Ian Talbot for guidance, and was advised to contact me. She wrote to me in March 1998 that her grandfather had gone to England for higher studies in early 1920s where he had an affair with her grandmother who gave birth to a girl child, her mother, after he had returned to India.

The young girl was brought up by her grandparents in a small Welsh village which was scandalized by the arrival of a parentless mixed-race child. Anyway, she grew up like other Welsh girls and settled down in life. For seventy-five years there was no talk of an Indian connection till Penny decided to explore her Indian roots and trace her Indian relations, the children and grandchildren of Inder Singh.

I surmised that a young Punjabi person going abroad for higher studies in the 1920s should most likely belong to one of the Punjab chief's family. So I wrote to Penny to go to the India Office library and consult the publication *Chiefs and Families of Note – Punjab*, which I had read in my student days. Lo and behold, my surmise turned out to be correct. It was discovered that Inder Singh did hail from a chief's family and was a professor in Khalsa College in 1940. Thereafter, I traced the family through my contacts and got the former's consent to own up Penny Thomson and her mother, daughter of Inder Singh. On my encouragement, Penny came to India with her mother in 1999 and I arranged for a family reunion in Delhi. Needless to say, my social service was greatly valued by Penny and her family.

Thus from a writer I turned into an author as well as a social historian.

19

An Obsession with the Raj Era

I COME FROM A GENERATION BORN and bought up during the heyday of the Raj. We studied *Simple Chapters of English Life*, a compulsory textbook for matriculation students. As regards the subject of history, our books had a chapter on 'Angrezi Raj ki Barkaten', or the blessings of English rule, and it was a standard question in school examinations. We generally thought of sahibs as Englishmen, though they included the Irish, Scots and Welsh; the word Britisher was seldom used. It was through the spread of modern education that English thought, literature and political tradition were introduced to India.

As I embarked on my writing career, my maiden project was *Nautch Girls of India*. The dancing girl as professional entertainer appears through the ages in different incarnations, from apsara in divine form, to ganika, devadasi, nartaki, kanchni, tawaif and finally to nautch girl during the Raj. I wanted to explore how and why the icon of performing arts called the nautch girl was banished from the entertainment scene by the end of the nineteenth century. For that it was important to study the social and cultural life of the sahibs and their accounts of nautch entertainment. I could not find any information about it in history books. So, I sought guidance of Dr P.J. Marshall, an eminent historian from London University. I had met him earlier during his visit to Delhi when he had given a lecture at the India International Centre (IIC). He was glad to note my zest for doing research on a topic no other scholar had done before. He advised me to explore the Raj literature, comprising journals, memoirs, diaries and travelogues by British scholars, travellers, officials and missionaries who had visited or lived in India during the eighteenth and nineteenth centuries.

From 1989 onwards, I earnestly started my study of Raj literature. I found some old books in the IIC library and the National Archives, but my ultimate destination for this research turned out to be India Office Library and Records, part of the British Library in London. I began my research with study of the massive four volumes of James Forbes's *Oriental Memoirs, Selected and Abridged from a Series of Familiar Letters Written during Seventeen Years Residence in India* (1813). Acclaimed as a classic of Raj literature, it is a kind of compendium of British knowledge about India. Rich in social and cultural reporting and enlivened with romantic and humorous anecdotes, these memoirs offer an eloquent description of beautiful Indian women and their costumes and jewels. There is also a delightful account of entertainment by nautch girls and musicians and their love songs. The nautch girls are described as 'extremely delicate in person, soft and regular in their features, with a form of perfect symmetry … preserve a decency and modesty in their demeanour which is more likely to allure than the shameless effrontery of similar characters in other countries'.

The other highly acclaimed classic of Raj literature is a monumental two-volume journal by Fanny Parks, the first Indophile memsahib, traveller, writer and artist. It is titled

Wanderings of a Pilgrim in Search of the Picturesque. Enamoured of India with its picturesque landscape and natural beauty, its people in exotic costumes, its festivals, music and dance, and even its cuisine, Fanny Parks is one of the most appealing chroniclers of Indian life and lifestyle in the first half of the nineteenth century. Little wonder, Fanny felt so much at home that she gives an absorbing account of a 'dazzling party with nautch girls and musicians' she attended at Calcutta. She also describes the performance of Nickec, then the most celebrated nautch girl of Calcutta, whom she called 'Catalina of the East'.

Another famous journal is the two-volume travelogue *Narrative of a Journey through Upper Provinces of India from Calcutta to Bombay* (1824–25) by Bishop Heber. He too was not immune to feminine charms as there are many references to pretty young women in his journal. He also describes nautch performances and admires their colourful costumes, adding that their dress was modesty itself, and nothing but their faces, feet and hands were visible.

I looked into scores of other journals and publications to gather more information and data about nautch girls–sahibs' impressions as patrons and spectators, their lifestyle, customs and manners, their role as singers, dancers and playmates and also the famous nautch girls of the Raj. I had by now sufficient material for my book.

Rich in historical and human interest, these journals and memoirs also provide a rare insight into the social and cultural life of the sahibs, who from traders had turned into empire builders. Embedded in its numerous volumes, I discovered revealing accounts of the changing pattern of the sahibs' lifestyle in India and how the early East India Company civilians and soldiers had come under the spell of Indian way of life. They took to hookah, arrack and Indian dress. They kept zenana, married native dusky beauties, and became fond of local sports of shikar, cockfights and other animal fights. They consulted astrologers and enjoyed nautch parties.

I got so much addicted to the Raj literature that I began visiting the British Library every year with a view to collecting material on the various aspects of the Raj or, so to say, untold stories from the Raj. I got particularly interested in the love life of the white community. The burgeoning Raj was very much a masculine affair. To rephrase a hoary catchphrase, the 'Empire was not acquired in a fit of absence of mind, so much as in a fit of absence of wives'. Deterred by the dangers of a long and tortuous voyage, few British women ventured to come to India, so up to beginning of the nineteenth century it was quite common for English settlers to keep an Indian bibi or mistress. It was amusing to find that an English editor of a local paper advised sahibs to sleep with Indian women to keep themselves cool in the beastly summer of Calcutta. There was nothing shameful or secret about these relationships, and even Governor General Sir John Shore and the governor of Bombay publicly kept native women. One Company official, Samuel Brown, recorded in his journal (c.1838): 'The native women are so amusingly playful, so anxious to please, that a person after being accustomed to their society shrinks from the idea of encountering the whims, or yielding to the furies of an English woman.' There was an army colonel who agreed to be circumcised in order to get possession of a Muslim woman who imposed this condition before becoming his mistress.

Towards the beginning of the nineteenth century, with the introduction of the overland route as well as steamships, British women started arriving in India in increasing numbers to hunt for husbands in the Indian marriage bazaar. They grew into a social phenomenon known as the fishing fleet. There are accounts of matches arranged on the spot while the venturesome beauties were on exhibition. As they were in search of husbands with wealth and position, many young girls married men twice their age who showered them with jewels, costly clothes and carriages to win their love. Many alliances were concluded in utter haste, without knowledge of the family background of prospective bridegrooms. Devoid of attachments, many such ill-matched unions led to illicit affairs and scandals. 'Young civil and military officials, without the financial means to afford a European wife, were ever willing to offer their services and pay their homage to the fashionable married women, who looked for amours outside wedlock.'

As the nineteenth century rolled on, the British established a chain of civil and military stations and their social life came to revolve within the community. They had their exclusive clubs for entertainment and enjoyment. As for their sex lives, it is difficult to determine the truth in the accusation that they committed adultery without compunction. At home, the Victorian standard of morality was quite strict. There was a general impression that British society in India was immoral and women were the target of most of the criticism. Husbands and wives spent long periods of time apart from each other, giving opportunities for extramarital affairs.

Flirting with the other sex was normal in British social life in India. Though considered a harmless game, there were occasions when it led to adultery followed by gossip and scandals. One regiment, known for its enthusiastic adultery, was labelled the 'Fornicating Fifth'. For sexual escapades of a more exciting kind there were hill stations which offered plenty of opportunity for fun to lonely wives and civil and military men on leave. Frank Richards, who served as an ordinary soldier in India before the World War I, felt that it was almost impossible for the young and pretty wife of a soldier to remain faithful to her husband if she were sent to the hills on her own. The open lifestyle in a close-knit community gave ample scope of rumours and gossip. It was proclaimed that the only way to keep adultery secret was to commit it on the night mail train.

In addition to the foregoing provocative information about the sex life of the sahibs as reported in journals and other Raj publications, I also came across fascinating love stories of sahibs and memsahibs of the period. With a view to recapturing the theme of love in all its glory and infamy, I selected twenty-three stories and presented them as they appeared in the original published texts except that some of them were given different titles and where required compressed for the sake of easy reading. My dear friend the late Raj Kakar helped me in preparing background notes to be appended at the beginning of the stories. Then I added an introduction covering the sahibs' sex life with bibis, mistresses concubines, whores and memsahibs. I sent the manuscript of *Love Stories from the Raj* to Penguin Books. They in turn passed it on to Khushwant Singh, their principal adviser, for approval. After receiving his nod they brought it out in 1995, thereby stimulating further my fancy for the Raj era. The book got copious reviews and became popular with the readers and continues to remain so even after twenty years with so many reprints, the last one in 2014.

Coming back to Raj literature, with increasing stability of the Raj and improved means of transport, more British people came to India in the latter half of the nineteenth century and recorded their experiences. It is also observed that many women authors were romantic diarists who delighted in reminiscences giving an autobiographical flavour to their writings. Next to Fanny Parks, there were Miss Emma Roberts, Mrs Graham, Mrs Kindersley, Mrs Elwood and Mrs Fenton who have all narrated their impressions of Hindu and Muslim festivals, their joint celebrations and also their distinctly separate mode of living. They have also recorded their estimation of Indian music and dance.

The journals are replete with accounts of luxurious life of the sahibs with an army of servants, palatial bungalows and the pageantry of official functions. There is ample information of people from different parts of India, their colourful costumes, their fairs and festivals, amusements with jugglers and snake charmers, caste and social order, thugs and robbers and the palanquin mode of transport. An interesting part is the authors' impressions of native women of different classes and regions of India. There are romanticized descriptions of women seen at the wells and river ghats. The authors of military professions are far more eloquent in recording the graceful appearance of exotic women with their supple figures and slender, well-rounded limbs. The maidens from the mountains hailed as 'daughters of nature' are extolled for their beauty and charm. All these delightful accounts inspired me to do other books on the Raj era, *Rare Glimpses of the Raj*, and *Stories from the Raj* and *Sahib's India – Vignettes from the Raj*.

Professor Talbot met me in Chicago with my friend Nazar Tiwana when he was working on the biography of his father Khizr Hayat Tiwana, the last premier of colonial Punjab. I acquainted him with my knowledge of the political situation in Punjab during that period. Later, he introduced me to Professor Denis Judd of North London University, an authority on British imperial history. He was impressed with my extensive research on the British period and my books on the Raj. Whenever I visited London, Professor Judd would invite me for giving lectures at his university on 'Untold Stories from the Raj'. Also, it was on his suggestion that Roger Bolton Productions, London, took me as a consultant for their documentary *Ruling Passions*. Apart from giving my interview on the nautch girls, I organized a nautch scene for them with the talented singer Vidya Rao and the accomplished

Kathak exponent Nandini in her gorgeous period costume. The documentary *Ruling Passions* depicts the sexual life of the sahibs, their attraction for nautch girls, their exploitation of Anglo-Indian women and the sad side of the sahibs' racial superiority. Later, Diverse Productions, London, took me as one of the consultants when they came to India for their documentary *Position Impossible: In Search of Kamasutra.* I explained the historical background of the institution of Indian courtesans as an integral part of culture from time immemorial. Accomplished in dance, music and the art of captivating men, she was patronized by the Indian elite as well as the sahibs.

The study of Raj literature impelled me to explore the vast pictorial record consisting of paintings, sketches and drawings of the period. British professional artists began arriving in India from the 1760s onwards in search of fame and fortune. While most of them concentrated on making portraits of the ruling elite, landscape painting or history pictures of imperial interest, there were others who applied their talents to depict the British way of life and the colour and diversity of India. Then there were Indian artists who were commissioned by British patrons to make pictures of Indian subjects.

Returning to my book *Nautch Girls of India*, I had finished the text. But I realized that no account of this nautch institution would be complete without plentiful illustrations. I recalled the old maxim: the pen may be mightier than the sword but the artist's brush is even mightier than the pen as the visual image can accomplish what words cannot. I had earlier collected a few images of nautch girls from the British Library and the Victoria and Albert Museum. Now I decided to enlarge my research by exploring the museums and galleries of both England and the USA. Fortunately, I got a complimentary Air India ticket for my research travel. Thanks to the guidance and help of Dr Mildred

Archer, the doyenne of historians of British art in India, I was able to accomplish my task by visiting the right sources – the British Library, Victoria and Albert Museum, Royal Asiatic Society, London; the US Library of Congress and the Yale Center of British Art, New Haven. These research visits also educated me about the vast amount of visual material on India held by these great institutions.

Finally, the day of jubilation arrived for me with the launch of my book in September 1996 by Khushwant Singh and Vasant Sathe, president Indian Council of Cultural Research. It was a colourful function at the ICC embellished with a dance performance by the renowned exponent of Vilasani Natyam, Swapanasundari. Sumptuously illustrated, *Nautch Girls of India* was highly acclaimed by the media with a spate of reviews and excerpts by leading newspapers and magazines. It was hailed as a pioneering work on the subject of dance and music as well as their practitioners through the centuries.

20

Other Writings

A REPRODUCTION OF THE FINEST PAINTINGS and drawings in my book *Nautch Girls of India* was highlighted in every book review. While researching in the museums and galleries abroad I had picked up a few images of Indian women by European artists and noted down details of their holdings on this subject. A study of Dr Mildred Archer's masterpiece *India and British Portraiture 1770-1825* revealed that some famous British professional artists had left behind not only charming portraits of nautch girls and Indian bibis but also paintings of ordinary women. I discovered in the illustrated publications of the Raj era a good amount of prints, aquatints, and lithographs portraying Indian women of different classes in their peculiar setting. *Swagat* magazine had earlier published my piece 'Early European Images of Indian Women'. All this inspired me to do a comprehensive study of the recorded impressions about Indian women by British observers as well as their visual images produced by the artists. I discussed this project with my old friend Jagmohan Mahajan, an art historian of the Raj period, who had earlier guided me in my research on the nautch girls. He encouraged me to go ahead and collect all the pictorial inputs from the identified sources abroad.

Already acquainted with the libraries, museums and galleries in England and the USA I wanted to collect this visual treasure. Though my stay abroad was taken care of in London by my son Rohit settled there and in the USA by generous friends, the air ticket was a costly affair. Besides, my earning from the book was so little that it did not even cover the cost of picture slides procured abroad, the publisher claiming to have run into a loss for unknown reasons. Having already enjoyed Air India's benevolence, I approached the ICCR for a research travel grant. Fortunately, *India Today* had just covered me on their newly introduced 'Author Speak Page'. Thanks to Foreign Secretary Salman Haidar, also the vice-president of the ICCR, I received the grant for visiting the UK and the USA to undertake research for my proposed book 'Indian Women through Foreign Eyes'.

I acquired visual material from the British Library and luckily the Victoria and Albert Museum gave me special permission to bring my own cameraman and take photographs of selected paintings. For me this was a great opportunity to collect a good number of pictures for my future use as well. I explored the National Portrait Gallery and Royal Collection as well and acquired a few interesting pictures. In the USA, my chief source was the Yale Center for British Art, New Haven.

This time, I spent many days in the US Library of Congress, Washington. Considering it to be my last visit to the USA I was anxious to make the best use of it. Earlier while researching in the library I had stumbled upon a fascinating eyewitness account of a nautch performance by an American writer, Lily S. Anderson, published in *ASIA: The American Magazine on the Orient*. I was now keen to study American writings on India and to my delight found in the bound volumes of *ASIA* several articles on India covering the political, economic, religious, social and cultural scene of the country during the early twentieth century. Founded in 1901, the journal had closed down in 1946. In the course of my exploration in the library I also discovered a vast collection of photographs of Indian monuments, cities and people in different walks of life. I was the first scholar to discover the fabulous collection of F.G. Carpenter, the noted American author and traveller, forgotten for nearly fifty years. Further, it was the first time that I saw stereograph picture cards and an enormous collection of these cards showing Indian landscapes, monuments, cities, people and the imperial durbars of Delhi. They had also kept an old device to view these picture cards in 3D form, presumably a predecessor of the view-master. This was indeed a rich treasure of India through the lens, in some ways even surpassing the British Library collection. We were allowed to snap the photographs or take Xerox prints. I did both and collected a good number of pictures of the Indian panorama of nearly a hundred years ago.

Back home, I began working on the text of my book now titled: *Beyond the Veil: Indian Women in the Raj*. I underlined the fact that women in India have always been accorded pride of place in both religious and philosophical thought. They were capable of advanced learning in every branch of knowledge, and enjoyed high status in society. This was followed by a long period when their status declined and they were relegated behind the veil. Coming to the Raj period, British authors have left behind fascinating accounts of Indian women and their customs and manners and mode of life. Armed with abundant material and a visual record comprising over a hundred illustrations, I completed the book in a year.

I was looking for a publisher for it when I met my American friend Lindsay Hebberd, a professional photographer, who had just done her book *Cultural Portraits of India* with the support of the Indian government. She had published it herself and got it printed by Ajanta Press. She advised me to get the book designed and a dummy made with the cover title along with a few pages of the text and some select illustrations. And with that I should seek government support. I did all that and courtesy my old friend and colleague Brajesh Mishra, then principal secretary to the prime minister, my book *Beyond the Veil*, the first work on the subject, won the support of the Ministry of External Affairs. They agreed to take five hundred copies for distribution to our missions abroad and for presentation. With this support and guidance from Lindsay Hebberd, I published the book on my own and had it printed at Ajanta Press. The book was launched in July 2000 by the then Union minister of state for external affairs, Ajit Kumar Panja, at a function organized by the XP Division at the IIC. Later, in December 2000, the book was launched at the Nehru Centre, London, by the Indian high commissioner. There was extensive media coverage with numerous reviews. The book was acclaimed as the first ever scholarly work of its kind on the formidable subject of the Indian woman and that too with rare illustrations obtained from collections all over the world. This was the first time that I made a tidy sum from my writing. Incidentally, the book also won an award for its quality production by the Federation of Indian Publishers at the Delhi Book Fair, 2001.

With abundant material on the Indian scene in the Raj including the visual record, I began contributing regularly to Indian newspapers and magazines. Furthermore, I wrote a series of articles on early European portrayal of women of Bengal, Punjab, Kashmir, Maharashtra and the mountain regions. The American embassy commissioned me to write about my discovery of Raj treasure in the US Library of Congress for *SPAN* magazine. It published my profusely illustrated articles, 'Frank G. Carpenter Collection', 'Raj Treasures in the Library of Congress' and

'American Soldiers in India'. It was editorially acknowledged that I was the first research scholar to discover this vast pictorial material on India in the US Library of Congress.

My published writings inspired some readers to communicate with me. They included PhD students and some senior citizens of Delhi. Some of the latter who had read my book on Lahore suggested that I should do a similar book on New Delhi. I too realized that much had been written about the historic city of Delhi but the story of the eighth city, the imperial New Delhi, its residents, the pattern of life and the social and cultural milieu of the Raj days remained a neglected field. So I prepared a project 'Echoes from Imperial New Delhi'. I wanted to cover not only the lifestyle of the ruling sahibs but more importantly the native staff residing in the DIZ Area, the Indian segment of New Delhi – a city within a city with its chain of squares. It was a beautiful garden town which was wiped out during the 1970s. The implementation of this project involved considerable research and study of contemporary published literature and unpublished diaries and memoirs, newspapers and magazines, as well as collecting oral information from surviving residents of those days. I approached Mrs Sheila Dikshit, then chief minister of Delhi, for sponsoring the project. She evinced great interest in the project but it was scuttled by her bureaucracy.

Around this time Mr Jagmohan, then minister of culture, got impressed with my published piece 'Indian Paintings in the Raj' and asked me to submit the proposal for a book on Indian artists of the Raj. So I prepared a project 'Marvels of Indian Painting – Rise and Demise of Company School'. It was to cover the achievements of Indian artists of the period, subject matters covered and novelties of painting on mica and ivory. Also, historical factors which led to the dominance of the Company School in the art scene of India for over a century and later its decline and disappearance from the scene. This was again a new field of research and the first coffee table book on the subject. My project was approved and I received a grant in 2002 from the Indira Gandhi National Centre for Arts for my research travel to Europe and the USA and to collect visual images from the galleries and museums there.

While working on this project, I was equally involved with another pursuit, the centenary celebrations of K.L. Saigal, immortal singer and superstar. I had already written quite a few pieces on K.L. Saigal and his music. The Ministry of Culture decided to sponsor the celebrations and appointed me as a coordinator. It was decided to produce a documentary on Saigal and a commemorative volume on his life and work in addition to musical concerts. I was given a grant for travel and research and the ministry undertook to buy five hundred copies for distribution to the libraries in India. I collected all the available photographs from the Film Archives, Pune, and other sources in Mumbai and Kolkata. With adequate experience after *Beyond the Veil,* I published an attractive volume *K.L. Saigal: Immortal Singer and Superstar*. It was launched by Jaipal Reddy, minister of culture, in 2004, the centenary year, at a colourful function organized by the ministry at the IIC. The book was highly acclaimed by the media in their numerous reviews.

With all this, my planned book *Marvels of Indian Painting* got delayed. While I had collected more than a hundred illustrations, it was now an uphill task to obtain waiver of the new high rates of reproduction fees introduced by the Victoria and Albert Museum. It took me more than a year and that too with the intervention of our high commissioner in London, Ronen Sen, that I obtained their waiver. Again I wanted to produce the book myself, and for that I needed some advance orders. Fortunately, both the Ministry of Culture and the Ministry External Affairs came to my rescue in 2006. This helped me bring it out the next year. It was launched by Dr Karan Singh, president, ICCR, in April 2007 at a function held at the British Council, New Delhi. Hailed as a pioneering work on the forgotten Indian artists, it received extensive coverage in many newspapers and magazines.

For the past so many years I was regularly contributing to my old favourite newspaper the *Tribune* especially after my friend Hari Jai Singh took over as editor followed by another dear friend, H.K. Dua, who earlier as editor of *Hindustan Times* had published quite a few of my writings. It was in late 2006 that I was commissioned by the Tribune Trust, courtesy H.K. Dua, to compile and update *Tribune 125 Years – An Anthology*. It was quite a laborious work but being a regular reader of the *Tribune* from student days I was excited and happy to be entrusted with this assignment. It was a herculean task and I spent several months in the Nehru Memorial Museum and Library peering through the *Tribune*'s old files. Anyway, I fulfilled my responsibility with full dedication which was duly appreciated when *Tribune 125 Years – An Anthology* was released by then prime minister, Dr Manmohan Singh, in May 2008.

I was now recognized by the book trade as an art historian and Raj specialist. Also, it came to be known that I was in possession of abundant rare visual material left behind by both British and Indian artists of the Raj period. Niyogi Books, an enterprising publisher of art books, approached me to do a richly illustrated book, *Raj Revisited*. I agreed to do it in my own way which involved a good amount of fresh writing. A novel feature of this project was that the publisher made an advance payment of Rs 50,000 to me. I worked hard to make an impressive volume, a virtual pilgrimage to the past and a guided tour of imperial India. I knew this would be my last art book. It was launched by my friend and colleague Natwar Singh at the IIC in November 2012 soon after my ninety-first birthday.

Back on my desk, I found that apart from my accumulation of photographs from the US Library of Congress, I had a good collection of American writings on India from the early twentieth century. It occurred to me to shape it into a book. I mentioned it to my old friend B.N. Varma of Primus Books and gave him my collection to evaluate its publication. He acknowledged that these writings were of great historic value and of much academic interest. He brought out an impressive hardcover *India through American Eyes:100 Years Ago*. It was launched by Dr Karan Singh at the IIC in September 2014.

21

Lahore Calling

THERE IS AN OLD SAYING, 'TO every bird its nest is best'. This explains why most people love the place where they were born or brought up. I belong to the vanishing generation of pre-Partition days who were forced to leave their homeland but carried 'Lahore' in their hearts like the memory of a first love. Overpowered by nostalgia, we still recall the days when Lahore had attained the reputation of being the 'Paris of the East' where people of different communities lived in harmony in the sunshine of their common heritage, historic bonds and flamboyant Punjabi culture.

No city in the subcontinent can boast of a more turbulent and stirring history or a stronger vitality than Lahore. In the heyday of its glory as the capital of the Mughals, the city rose from semi-obscurity to eminence. It finds mention in English poet Milton's classic, 'Paradise Lost'. Rudyard Kipling, the Nobel laureate who was raised in Lahore, immortalized the city in his writings. During the Raj, Lahore emerged as the fortress and jewel of the Indian Empire.

Lahorias have extraordinary attachment to their city and evince immense pride in belonging to it. So much so, the obituary columns of Indian newspapers until the 1980s carried the announcement reporting the deceased as so and so formerly of Lahore. No wonder, every Punjabi would proclaim: '*Jine Lahore nahin dekhya, oh jamya hi nahin*' (One who has not seen Lahore is as good as not having been born at all). Scripted by Dr Asghar Wajahat, a noted Hindi writer, the play with the same title – *Jine Lahore* – was first staged in Delhi in 1990. Its unprecedented popularity took the play to Pakistan, the UK, the USA, and all over India. The number of shows has exceeded one thousand in different languages. The play communicates an omnipresent fact – human emotions are the same everywhere and across all territorial cultural and national boundaries. A classic case of someone's incredible devotion to his hometown pertains to the saga of Lahore in America. A village in Orange County, Virginia, in the USA, was named Lahore in the 1850s by the owner of a general store after reading a book about India. A Pakistani Lahoria, Mr Noor Naghmi, brought the American Lahore in news in 2007 when he bought 235 acres of this township for $3 million. He wanted to turn it into an attractive tourist hub with reflections of his hometown Lahore's panorama.

Around 1990, along with some old schoolmates from Lahore, Dr Prem Sobti, Sudarshan Khanna, R.G.Nayyar, Jagmohan Mahajan and I formed the Lahore Club. Now retired and in our late sixties and seventies, we started meeting every day from 11.30 a.m. to 1 p.m. at the India International Centre lounge. We would amuse ourselves talking about the good old days in Lahore and sharing memories of the past. A favourite topic was to compare everything in our daily life at Delhi to that of Lahore in our days, followed by praise of the British art of governance which ensured law and order. Within a year a few more old contemporaries in Lahore joined us and the club now had twelve members.

We introduced a monthly lunch on a contributory basis but a suggestion to include wives was rejected by the life president, Dr Prem Sobti. He however accepted another proposal from R.G. Nayyar to have the members' birthday cocktail parties. Being a widower and living alone, Mr Nayyar offered his place at 41 Privthviraj Road for these get-togethers. We took his offer gladly and his place came to be designated as the 'Lahore Baithak'. We had numerous booze parties there over the years, even entertaining some Pakistani friends coming from Lahore. Twenty-five years have gone by, and most of the members have departed like all other Lahorias for their heavenly abode. We are only three survivors from the original group, P.L. Lamba (ninety-six), Prakash Kapur (ninety-one) and myself (ninety-three). There are two entrants, Dr Harish Khosla (ninety-four) and Dr Mani Talwar (eighty-seven). We still try to meet two to three times a week at the same spot in the IIC and continue to be hailed by everyone as the 'Lahore Club'.

My emotional attachment to Lahore found expression in my book, *Lahore: A Sentimental Journey* (1993). I had received quite a few invitations from my pen friends to visit but the right opportunity came in 1997 when my friends P.L. Lamba of the Kwality group and Pyarelal asked me to join them on their visit there to attend a wedding in their friend Kaisar Monnoo's family. It was after fifty years that I set foot on the soil of my beloved city. The first glimpse of the city from the plane presented a delightful sight of a metropolis with a vast expanse of glittering lights, a glaring contrast to the old image of Lahore in my mind which had haunted me all these years. One reason for not visiting Lahore earlier was my earnest desire to preserve in my mind the images of the social and cultural scene of Lahore of my days for reproducing these in my book.

The most thrilling part of my visit was meeting my old friend and classmate Saeed Ahmad Khan, particularly as I had been misinformed that he was no more. While dedicating my book on Lahore to the memory of my old friends, I had included his name as well. I tore off the dedication page before giving him a copy of my book. He noticed it and when I told him the reason behind it, he was vastly amused. It was a touching encounter that released the floodgates of memories. Though meeting after an interval of half a century I felt as if we had separated only the day before. I vividly recall my first day in Government College in 1937 when I had met Saeed and struck up a friendship with him. And now we sat down to celebrate the diamond jubilee of this friendship after missing both the silver and the golden ones. Supplemented by a bottle of excellent Scotch, our jubilee celebrations carried on till dawn.

We recalled the exciting visits to Hira Mandi where we went to hear Tamancha Jan, the famous singer of Lahore. I was delighted to learn that she was still alive and leading a retired life. The next day Saeed took me to her place, a tiny tenement near the Model Town area of Lahore. Meeting Tamancha Jan after over fifty years was a memorable experience. A singer nonpareil, now forgotten, she was the reigning queen of song during the 1940s at Hira Mandi. I had preserved the image of Tamancha Jan's youth and was somewhat shocked to see her ailing, shrunken frame, but as we began talking of the good old times, the twinkle in her eyes returned and she began narrating her experiences when she was a famous artiste in Lahore and an object of envy. She recalled the Lahore of pre-Partition days and said in a disconsolate voice, 'Practically all my patrons left Lahore after Partition and so I stopped singing and shut down my salon.'

Her educated daughter, who had in the meanwhile dropped in with her husband, confirmed this and praised her mother. She emphasized that not only was she proud of her mother for all she had done to bring up her children but unlike others, she had absolutely no hesitation in acknowledging her antecedents. I was pleasantly surprised and mightily pleased by the young lady's courageous and fearless statement. Tamancha Jan was visibly moved and gave a broad smile before bidding us farewell. 'Khuda hafiz,' she said and asked me to come and see her again on my next visit to Lahore.

The visit to my school, DAV, now Muslim High School No. 2, was also a moving experience. The familiar faces of teachers and classmates loomed before my eyes transporting me back to the 1930s when I studied there. It was interesting to find that the school building stood exactly as it was over fifty years earlier except that the swimming pool had vanished. From there I walked up to my alma mater, Government College, now a university. As I was walking around the building, someone came up and invited me to see the principal, Dr Khalid Aftab. I was delighted to meet Dr Aftab, an impressive personality with pleasant manners. Learning that I was an old student of the college and now a writer and author, he requested me to come and address the students. We exchanged notes about college activities then and now. The front view of the college complex looked as imposing as before. The only notable addition was the mosque on the left of the main Gothic structure.

Another highlight of the Lahore pilgrimage was my maiden visit to Government House where, courtesy some friends, I joined a luncheon party given by the governor, Shahid Hamid. The Lahore Government House, one of the palaces of the Raj, was acclaimed as the biggest and the best in India. I recall we could hardly see anything as the main building lay hidden among the trees in its enormous compound behind a high fortress-like wall topped with broken glass. The only thing visible of this forbidden mysterious world used to be the Union Jack hoisted on the octagonal tower.

My friend Dr Ajaz Anwar took me to the famous Mayo School

of Art, now upgraded to National College of Art. I enjoyed interacting there with the principal, teachers and students. It was a pleasant sight to find young boys and girls listening to music and sketching or sculpting. I was told by one of them that this was the most noteworthy location of the vanished veils in the city. There I also met Prof. Iqbal Hussain, the world-famous Pakistani artist whose rise from street punk to painter was splashed by *Time* magazine and whose works were sold at Sotheby's and Christie's. This noble artist proudly proclaims his lineage from a courtesan's family of Hira Mandi.

My next visit to Lahore was in 1999 to enjoy the famous Basant festival celebrations there. This time I stayed with my pal Saeed Ahmad and spent more time with his family. An ardent kite flier myself, I was thrilled to see countless colourful kites in the sky. A major novelty of the extravagant festivities with dance and music was night kite flying, unheard of in my days. The kites with luminous strings floating in the starry skies presented a wonderful sight along with fireworks and even gunshots to announce their victory in kite fighting matches. As the night advanced, I saw more people coming to the rooftops along with Bhangra teams dancing to Indian film music and the beating of drums. The female participants in this gaiety and hilarity were an added attraction with their fancy costumes in yellow hue. This enchanting spectacle was then hailed as the only one of its kind in the entire world. No wonder, it had emerged as the greatest tourist attraction for Lahore.

The passing away of my old pal Saeed Ahmad in 2000 was a rude shock for me especially when he was all set to come to Delhi and stay with me in December the same year. Missing him I did not go to Lahore for a few years. It was in 2005 that I went to attend the annual function of the Government College 'Old Students' Union'. Later in the year I was invited by Dr

Khalid Aftab, vice chancellor, Government College University, to participate in the first 'International History Conference' on 'Punjab and the Raj'. I attended the two-day conference held at Lahore in January 2006 and presented a paper, 'Imperial Lahore in the Raj'. Other participants included learned historians from Pakistan and abroad including my friend Prof. Ian Talbot who had now moved over from Coventry to Southampton University.

By this time I had become friends with M.P. Bhandara, owner of the famous Murree Brewery and also a senator. He made frequent visits to Delhi and spent a lot of time with me at the IIC. Interestingly, once he hosted a big bash at the Foreign Correspondents' Club for introducing his single malt whiskey in the Delhi market. A perfect gentleman, full of life, he turned into an additional attraction for my visiting Lahore, more so when he insisted that I should stay at his Lahore guest house. Whenever I went, he would join me from Rawalpindi and organize splendid gatherings which enlarged my circle of friends at Lahore.

I even took my grandchildren to Lahore for some friends' family weddings. In 2010, I was invited to the International Conference on Sufism and Peace at Islamabad. The three-day conference attended by writers, poets and intellectuals from thirty-five countries resolved to promote peace, interfaith harmony, pluralism and reconciliation to counter terrorism. On my return I broke my journey and spent a few days in Lahore.

Government College University began inviting me every year on the Annual Founder's Day as their guest of honour. The Ajoka Theatre, with whom I had a long association, made me chairman of the 'Theatre for Peace Committee' with members from both Pakistan and India. Incidentally, I am reminded of an amusing episode about Ajoka Theatre's special showing of one of their Punjabi plays for the then Indian prime minister, I.K. Gujral.

After the play Mr Gujral just held Madeeha Gauhar and patted her appreciatively for producing a great play. The photograph showing both of them led to a controversy in Pakistan and Madeeha Gauhar was taken to court by lawyers in Lahore for appearing in a photograph where she seems to be embracing the Indian prime minister. Interestingly, a Lahore judge instead of dismissing the case as frivolous decided to serve notice to Madeeha Gauhar. This was followed by another crackpot in Karachi who went to court accusing her of dancing with the Indian prime minister.

Later in 2010, I came into the limelight when my late friend Saeed Ahmad's granddaughter Zulekha, a freelance journalist who had met me at Islamabad, wrote a long piece titled 'Saeed and Pran – Friends for Life'. This was published by Pakistan's the *News* in 'Aman Ki Asha – Destination Peace' series launched by the *Times of India* and the Jung Group of Pakistan. By now quite a few media persons came to know of me, and every time I was in Lahore, someone would come up to interview me, usually about my days in Lahore and Indo-Pak common heritage in art and culture. I appeared quite a few times on the Lahore local TV channel as well. Invariably, they would ask me about my attachment to Lahore. My answer was simple, 'Lahore, Lahore hai – it defies description, it can only be felt and experienced.'

The popularity of literary festivals in the subcontinent inspired a bright young entrepreneur, Razi Ahmed, to ensure that Lahore does not lag behind in this field. I was invited to the inaugural Lahore Literary Festival held in February 2013. I took part in the panel discussion on 'Lahore in Literature' along with eminent writers Bapsi Sidhwa and Intizar Hussain. The festival was well organized and a great success. Later, in response to an invitation, I participated in the International Peace Conference organized by the World Punjabi Congress and International Sufi Council held at Lahore in December 2013. The conference highlighted the role of participating scholars, intellectuals and writers for the establishment of peaceful relations among countries. As nearly half the participants were from India, the emphasis was on greater peace, harmony and friendship between India and Pakistan and strengthening of trade and economic relations. I too spoke about our common heritage in art and literature and received a standing ovation when the chairman, Fakhar Zaman announced that I was ninety-plus with roots in Lahore.

The following year opened with my visit to Lahore in January for chairing the 'Theatre for Peace' meeting there. It was also an occasion for the celebration of Ajoka Theatre's thirteenth anniversary when they launched their new play *Lo Phir Basant Ayee*. It is a powerful satire clamouring for social justice and challenging the extremism and tolerance bigotry that led to the banning of Basant celebration and kite flying. Citing my memories of Basant in Lahore culled from my book *Lahore: A Sentimental Journey*, the play *Lo Phir Basant Ayee* has been dedicated to me.

I was again invited to participate in the Lahore Literary Festival, 2014. In addition to the regular Lahore session, I joined the panel discussion on 'Amrita Sher-Gil – Lahore's Lost Daughter'. Further, there was an interesting interaction with Tehmina Durrani, the celebrated author of the classic *My Feudal Lord*. She presented me an autographed copy of her latest book, *Happy Things in Sorrow Times*.

Later in the year, in November, I was invited to take part in the Thap (Trust for History, Art and Culture, Pakistan) Conference held at Lahore. A non-profit trust established in 2006 by Prof. Pervaiz Vandal, an architect, and his wife Sajida Vandal, former principal, National College of Art, Thap is a forum of academics and professionals dedicated to improving the state of education, particularly in the field of art and culture. Their acclaimed book on Bhai Ram Singh, the first Indian principal of Mayo School of Art, was released by me at Delhi in 2007. This year the conference's theme was 'Culture, Art and Architecture of the Marginalized and the Poor'. Both Pakistani and foreign scholars contributed to the deliberations of the conference.

I hope Lahore will continue calling me.

22

Celebration of People's Music: The K.L. Saigal Memorial Circle

MUSIC IS GOD'S GREATEST GIFT TO mankind. It is not merely a means of entertainment but also perhaps the most effective instrument for sublime communion with the ultimate. In ancient India, music was mostly interwoven with the religious and ritualistic part of life. One of the earliest forms of Indian classical music was 'Dhrupad', tracing its origin to the Sama Veda. The advent of Islam introduced the Persian, Arabic and Central Asian elements into Indian classical music. The temple Dhrupad then moved into royal courts and emerged as 'khayal gayaki' with compositions becoming more secular in nature. This was followed by light classical forms such as the Thumri, Dadra and ghazal but all based on classical ragas.

The advent of recording in the early twentieth century marked the dawn of a new era. The accomplished professional singers emerged as gramophone singers like Gauhar Jan of Calcutta, Malka Jan of Agra, Sundarabai of Poona and Jankibai of

Allahabad. Their popular songs, bhajans and ghazals reached the masses as people's music.

It was the introduction of talkies with the release of *Alam Ara* in 1931 that brought another revolution in the world of Indian music. The songs for the first talkies were usually taken from the stage dramas based on classical music. Later, however, the film music evolved its own form and style and turned into the most popular form of people's music. New Theatres of Calcutta were the pioneers in introducing a totally new form of film music based on traditional ragas but fused with popular folk tunes. The founding fathers of this genre of people's music were eminent music directors – R.C. Boral, Pankaj Mallick, Timir Baran and Kamal Dasgupta. Then there was a great musical genius K.L. Saigal with a heavenly voice, who became an icon of people's music. The one voice which is still popular is that of Saigal who is hailed as the modern-day Tansen.

My passion for music dates back to childhood. Instead of telling tales to make me sleep, my mother would sing bhajans narrating episodes from the Ramayana. As I grew up, I enjoyed listening to gramophone records of popular Punjabi songs. Then as a college student, like all others, I was drawn towards film music. My devotion to music even inspired me to join the Gandharv Mahavidyalay in Lahore to learn playing the violin. I vividly remember cycling down on Ravi Road every morning during the summer vacations in 1939. I learnt to play a couple of film tunes on my violin and got so much involved that I was humming the notes all the time. However, I was persuaded by my father to give up this hobby for later years and devote myself to studies.

My interest in music continued and I joined the students' Amateur Allied Arts Circle as secretary. We organized musical concerts at the Open Air Theatre in Lawrence Gardens, Lahore. The most memorable one was to raise funds for the war efforts.

With a recommendation letter from the Punjab chief justice, Douglas Young, we went to Noor Jehan's house to solicit her taking part in the concert, but her mother considered her too young for the stage and sent her elder daughter Iddan to sing for us.

A decade later, most of my friends from Lahore were settled in Delhi, including my wealthy pal from schooldays Bawa Sunder Singh, who was equally fond of music. During the 1950s, thanks to Naina Devi, an outstanding exponent of classical music, we had several private mehfils with noted singers at his house in Sunder Nagar until his untimely demise in 1961.

Later, I associated myself with the Raag-Rang Society set up by Naina Devi, also a great patron of artists. Her home in Kaka Nagar was a Mecca for musicians from every corner of India and Pakistan. I attended many concerts over the years at her house and got acquainted with a number of accomplished artists. After her passing away in 1993, I resolved to do something positive to propagate people's music and promote young talented artists. As a dedicated fan of K.L. Saigal, I wrote a few articles on Saigal and his music and followed it up with illustrated talks on Saigal's birth anniversaries at the IHC and IIC. I was enthused to find the swelling audience of Saigal fans and this turned me into the founder convener of K.L. Saigal Memorial Circle.

In January 2003 I was invited by the Nehru Centre, Mumbai, where I made an audio-visual presentation, 'K.L. Saigal – Life and Times'. I persuaded the Ministry of Culture to celebrate the centenary of K.L. Saigal in 2004, which was done with a ceremonial concert inaugurated by the then minister Jaipal Reddy. K.L. Saigal Memorial Circle organized a number of events during the centenary year 2004–05 including one at the Nehru Centre, London.

A notable event of the centenary celebrations was the presentation of a unique fusion of Saigal's poetry and music with a dance performance by renowned Kathak exponent Shovana Narayan. This unparalleled exposition received wide publicity and we were invited by the Nehru Centre, Mumbai, to repeat the performance.

During the past fifteen years, nearly a hundred musical functions have been organized under the aegis of K.L. Saigal Memorial Circle to honour the memory of most of the great singers of the twentieth century – Pankaj Mallick, Mukesh, Mohd Rafi, Talat Mahmood, Hemant Kumar, Manna Dey, Noor Jehan, Geeta Dutt, Suraiya, Malka, Pukhraj and Shamshad Begum. The celebrities of the gramophone era – Gauhar Jan, Sundarabai, Jankibai, Kamla Jharia and Juthika Roy – were duly saluted with memorial functions. Furthermore, I published a number of articles on the life and times of these eminent artists. Due reverence has also been extended to eminent music directors, the creators of hit melodies, like R.C. Boral, S.D. Burman, Khemchand Prakash, O.P. Nayyar, Madan Mohan, Roshan and Naushad.

People usually remember the singer and the song but not the poet or lyricist who produced it with his head and heart. We have paid homage to the famous lyricists Kedar Sharma, D.N. Madhok, Sahir Ludhianvi and Shakeel Badayuni. As regards poets, most of the eminent Urdu poets of the subcontinent were remembered with concerts of their poetry and music. For Hafeez Jullundhri, Sir Mohd Iqbal and Faiz Ahmad Faiz, special functions were held blending poetry, music and dance, with performing artists like Radhika Chopra, an acclaimed singer, and Rani Khanam, a renowned Kathak exponent.

To promote and popularize 'ghazal gayaki', a two-day ghazal festival was organized in collaboration with ICCR in 2013. The four artistes who gave their performance at Azad Bhavan were Rashmi Agarwal, Seema Anil Sehgal, Gaurav Sood and Radhika Chopra.

Ghazal Queen Begum Akhtar's centenary (2014–15) was celebrated with functions at Epicentre, Gurgaon, IIC and IHC On this occasion a special album carrying my private recording of Begum Akhtar done in 1958 at a private mehfil was released by her foremost disciple, Vidushi Shanti Hiranand.

Another unforgettable event held in May 2015 at Epicenter, Gurgaon, as well as IIC was 'The Courtesan: An Enigma' based on my book. The concert featured the renowned Sufi Kathak exponent Manjari Chaturvedi performing Darbari Kathak, the dance of the courtesan, known for its delicate movements and expressions.

In the world of music, we share a common heritage with Pakistan, both in classical as well as people's music. The icons of India and Pakistan, K.L. Saigal and Noor Jehan, are adored and intently listened to by millions of fans on both sides of the border. So are the present-day singers who are popular in both countries, with a common repertoire of popular ghazals. Coming to films, many of them with the same titles have been produced by both sides. Next, there are songs with similar theme and words, and traditional Punjabi songs converted into Hindi/Urdu with same tunes. There are also instances of the same lyrics in Indian and Pakistani films. A compilation of video clips covering these common elements was converted into a documentary, *Indo-Pak Musical Journey*, which was shown a few times with musical concerts devoted to this theme. The popularity of our functions at IIC and IHC had already earned me the Doordarshan title of 'Gunijan' after it interviewed me. This time, as requested by DD Bharti, I made a special documentary for them titled *Indo-Pak Musical Journey* which was broadcast in two slots: 'Sanjhi Virasat' and 'Bharat-Pakistan Sangeet Yatra.'

There is ample patronage, both official and by the corporate sector, for classical music and its exponents but there is no support for the people's music and 'ghazal gayaki'. Through its musical functions K.L. Saigal Memorial Circle tries to keep alive the memory of the forgotten greats of the Indian music world by encouraging young artists to pay shraddhanjali to them and also entertain the new generation of music lovers. A number of artists associated with us, like Dr Radhika Chopra, Shevanti Sanyal, Rashmi Agarwal, Priya Kanungo, Anjuman Saxena, Dr Meelu Verma, Dr Gaurav Sood and some others are now well-known not only in Delhi but even in other cities and abroad in West Asia, the UK and the USA. The popularity of our functions has inspired and encouraged a number of other organizers in Delhi and elsewhere to hold functions for 'Bhule Bisre Geet', in the memory of great icons like Mohd Rafi, Mukesh, Kishore Kumar and others. All these musical gatherings mark the celebration of people's music.

Index